BEYOND LOSS:
REBUILDING FROM THE ASHES

ONESIMUS MALATJI

Copyright © 2023 ONESIMUS MALATJI
All rights reserved.

Beyond loss: Rebuilding from the ashes

By: Onesimus Malatji

Copyright ©2023 by Onesimus Malatji
Cover Design by CiX Connect
Interior Design by CiX Connect

Trademark Notice:

All trademarks mentioned within this book belong to their respective owners.

All rights reserved. No part of this publication may be reproduced, distributed, or transmitted in any form or by any means, including photocopying, recording, or other electronic or mechanical methods, without the prior written permission of the publisher, except in the case of brief quotations embodied in critical reviews and certain other non-commercial uses permitted by copyright law.

For permissions requests, contact the publisher at:
ony@cixconnect.co.za

Copyright Violation Warning:
Unauthorized reproduction or distribution of copyrighted material is against the law. Any unauthorized copying, distribution, or use of material from this book may result in legal action.
Fair Use Notice: This book may contain copyrighted material used for educational and illustrative purposes. Such material is used under the "fair use" provisions of copyright law.

Disclaimer:
The information provided in this book is for general informational purposes only. The author and publisher are not offering legal, financial, or professional advice. Readers are advised to consult appropriate professionals for advice specific to their individual situations.
Accuracy Disclaimer: While every effort has been made to ensure the accuracy of the information presented in this book, the author and publisher cannot be held responsible for any errors, omissions, or inaccuracies.

Fair Use Notice: This book may contain copyrighted material used for educational and illustrative purposes. Such material is used under the "fair use" provisions of copyright law.

Third-Party Content:

This book may reference or include content from third-party sources. The author and publisher do not endorse or take responsibility for the accuracy or content of such third-party material.

Endorsements:

Any endorsement, testimonial, or representation contained in this book reflects the author's personal views and opinions. It does not imply an endorsement by any third party.
Results Disclaimer: The success stories and examples mentioned in this book are not guarantees of individual success. Actual results may vary based on various factors, including effort and circumstances.

Results Disclaimer:

The success stories and examples mentioned in this book are not guarantees of individual success. Actual results may vary based on various factors, including effort and circumstances.
No Guarantee of Outcome: The strategies, techniques, and advice provided in this book are based on the author's experiences and research. However, there is no guarantee that following these strategies will lead to a specific outcome or result.

Fair Use Notice:

This book may contain copyrighted material used for educational and illustrative purposes. Such material is used under the "fair use" provisions of copyright law.

ACKNOWLEDGMENTS

I extend my deepest gratitude to everyone who has been a part of this incredible journey, both seen and unseen. Your support, encouragement, and unwavering belief in me have been the driving force behind the creation of this book.

To my family, for standing by me through thick and thin, for believing in my dreams, and for being a constant source of inspiration – your love and encouragement have been my guiding light.

To my friends, mentors, and colleagues, your valuable insights and feedback have shaped the ideas within these pages. Your willingness to share your wisdom and experiences has enriched this work beyond measure.

To all those who have supported me on my path, whether through a kind word, a helping hand, or a moment of shared understanding, thank you. Your presence in my life has made all the difference.

To the countless individuals who have faced challenges and setbacks, yet continued to strive for greatness, your stories have fuelled the inspiration behind these words. May you find solace and encouragement within these pages.

And finally, to the readers who have embarked on this journey with me, thank you for allowing me to share my thoughts and experiences. It is my hope that this book serves as a beacon of hope, a source of guidance, and a reminder that fulfilment can be found in every step of life's intricate tapestry.

With heartfelt appreciation,

Onesimus Malatji

BEYOND LOSS:
REBUILDING FROM THE ASHES

TABLE OF CONTECT   PAGES

1: The Silent Corridors of High School 12-14
2: Solitude and the Birth of Curiosity 15-16
3: The World of Electronics 17-18
4: Dreams Deferred: College Challenges 19-21
5: The Unfulfilled Path of Mechanical Engineering 22-23
6: Turning to Information Technology 24-25
7: The Dropout: A New Beginning 26-27
8: The Old 486DX4: A Blessing in Disguise 28-29
9: Facing Mockery and Doubt 30-31
10: Self-Education: A Journey Begins 32-33
11: The Power of DOS 34-35
12: Meeting Amos: A New Mentor 36-37
13: The Struggle with Commands 38-39
14: A Dream's Command: The Turning Point 40-41
15: Fixing the Unfixable 42-43
16: Molefe: A Friend and Collaborator 44-45
17: The Birth of a Business Partnership 46-47
18: The First Big Project 48-49
19: Rising Tensions: The Split 50-51
20: The Path of Teaching and Sharing Knowledge 52-53
21: Compugem: A New Alliance 54-55
22: The Breakdown of a Partnership 56-57
23: Loxion Onys Printing Agency: The Start 58-59
24: Entering the World of Graphic Design 60-61
25: A Lie Turned Opportunity 62-63
26: Mastering Corel Draw 64-65
27: The Business of Creativity 66-67
28: Sosha Times and Africa Ntshebele 68-69
29: The Birth of Street is Waar 70-71
30: Cybercafe: A Community Haven 72-73
31: Expansion: The Durban Adventure 74-75
32: The Split of ONY LE EDY 76-77
33: Cyber Influx: A New Identity 78-79
34: Entering Telecommunications 80-81
35: The Challenge of Remote Connectivity 82-83
36: Sabotage: Battling the Unexpected 84-85
37: The MTN South Africa Partnership 86-87

38: Dreams Unravel: The Partnership Fails 88-89
39: Writing: A New Chapter 90-91
40: The Journey to 147 Books 92-93
41: Embracing the Digital Age 94-95
42: Life's Unpredictable Nature 96-97
43: The Burden of Loss 98-99
44: Relearning the Business World 100-101
45: Navigating Through Industry Manipulation 102-103
46: The Perils of Envy and Betrayal 104-105
47: The Power of Creating and Innovating 106-107
48: Rising Like a Phoenix 108-109
49: Overcoming Life's Demons 110-111
50: The Struggle with Licensing and Regulations 112-113
51: The Weight of Financial Burdens 114-115
52: Rediscovering Purpose 116-117
53: The Drive for Fulfilment 118-119
54: The Void of Loss 120-121
55: Confronting Death and Legacy 122-123
56: Building a Life Beyond Material Success 124-125
57: Redefining Success in Business 126-127
58: The Entrepreneur's Resilience 128-129
59: A New Vision for the Future 130-131
60: The Essence of Innovation 132-133
61: Learning from Past Mistakes 134-135
62: The Path of a Serial Entrepreneur 136-137
63: Facing Uncertainty with Courage 138-139
64: The Art of Reinvention 140-141
65: The Gift of Empowering Others 142-143
66: Leaving a Lasting Impact 144-145
67: Reflections on a Life's Journey 146-147
68: Beyond the Ashes: A New Dawn 148-149
69: The Ultimate Ascent: Looking Forward 150-151
70. Epilogue 152-153
71. Afterword 154-155

BEYOND LOSS:

REBUILDING FROM THE ASHES

PROLOGUE

As we open the pages to the remarkable story of Onesimus Malatji, we are invited to embark on a journey that traverses the multifaceted landscape of entrepreneurship, resilience, and personal growth. This prologue serves as a gateway into the life of a man whose journey transcends the mere act of building businesses, touching the very core of what it means to be a visionary, a leader, and a changemaker.

Onesimus Malatji's story begins not at the inception of his first business venture but in the roots of his early life experiences, shaping his character and his approach to the world of entrepreneurship. His beginnings are humble, marked by challenges and circumstances that forged in him a resilience and determination that would become the hallmark of his entrepreneurial spirit.

From his earliest forays into business, driven by a mix of necessity and ambition, Onesimus displayed an innate ability to identify opportunities and a fearless approach to seizing them. His journey is a vivid illustration of entrepreneurship as a continuous process of learning, adapting, and overcoming obstacles.

This prologue sets the stage for a narrative that is as much about personal transformation as it is about business success. It introduces us to the key themes that will recur throughout Onesimus's story: the importance of adaptability and lifelong learning, the value of resilience in the face of failure, and the profound impact of empowering others and giving back to the community.

As we delve into the chapters of Onesimus's life, we are reminded that his story is not just a chronicle of business ventures but a larger narrative about the power of human potential. It's a story that inspires and challenges us to look beyond our limitations, to embrace the journey with all its highs and lows, and to always strive for a greater purpose in our endeavours.

The prologue to Onesimus Malatji's story invites readers to not just observe but to engage with a journey that is rich in lessons and insights. It's an invitation to explore the depths of what it means to be an entrepreneur in the fullest sense – not just in business, but in life.

THE SILENT CORRIDORS OF HIGH SCHOOL

In the small, bustling town where Onesimus Malatji grew up, the high school stood as a beacon of youth and promise. But for Onesimus, its corridors whispered a different story. They were silent, echoing with the unspoken thoughts of a young boy who walked them alone.

High school for many is a time of vibrant social interactions and lifelong friendships, but for Onesimus, it was a journey marked by solitude. He was the quiet one, often overlooked, labelled as uninteresting by his more vibrant classmates. Where laughter and chatter filled the air, he found himself enveloped in an invisible cloak of isolation.

This loneliness was not just a physical reality but an emotional landscape he navigated daily. The rejection stung, leaving a mark on his young mind. But in this solitude, Onesimus found something unexpected - a refuge in his own thoughts, a space where his mind wandered freely, untethered by the constraints of peer acceptance.

It was in these silent corridors that Onesimus's curiosity began to take root. Devoid of the usual teenage distractions, he turned his attention to the world of electronics. This wasn't a choice born out of a plethora of options but a necessity - a way to fill the void left by the absence of companionship.

His interest in electronics started as a mere hobby, a way to pass the long hours after school. But soon, it grew into something more - a passion. He would spend hours dismantling old radios, fascinated by the maze of circuits and wires. Each component he uncovered was like a piece of a puzzle, waiting to be understood and put back together.

This hobby quickly turned into a self-taught journey. Onesimus found solace in the pages of electronics magazines and books, absorbing information that was worlds away from his high school curriculum. He was not just learning about electronics; he was learning how to learn - independently, methodically, and with a deep sense of purpose.

As Onesimus moved through the silent corridors of his high school, his mind was alive with plans and possibilities. Each day, he grew more distant from the world of his peers, but closer to the world he was creating for himself. In these formative years, the seeds of an innovator were sown.

His high school years, though lonely, were a crucible that forged his character. They taught him resilience, the value of self-reliance, and the power of curiosity. As he walked out of the school gates for the last time, Onesimus was not just leaving behind a place of learning; he was stepping into a future that he had started to mould with his own hands.

In "The Silent Corridors of High School," we witness the early shaping of a mind that would one day navigate the complex world of business and innovation. It was in these quiet moments of solitude that Onesimus Malatji began his unwitting journey towards becoming an entrepreneur.

SOLITUDE AND THE BIRTH OF CURIOSITY

As the high school years of Onesimus Malatji came to a close, the solitude that once felt like a heavy cloak began to transform into a mantle of discovery. This chapter of his life, devoid of the typical high school camaraderie, became the fertile ground where his curiosity and love for electronics took root and flourished.

In the quiet of his own company, Onesimus discovered a world far beyond the walls of his classroom. His fascination with electronics wasn't born out of a desire to join the ranks of hobbyists; it was a response to the silent conversations he had with himself in the empty corridors of his school. Where others found discomfort in solitude, Onesimus found freedom – freedom to explore, to think, and to dream.

His home became a sanctuary where he could delve deeper into his newfound interest. Old radios, discarded electronics, and any gadget he could lay his hands on became his companions. He learned not from teachers or structured courses, but from the silent language of circuits and wires. Each device he dismantled and reassembled was a lesson in patience, a lesson in understanding the intricate dance of electronics.

This self-education was not without its challenges. Onesimus often hit roadblocks, moments where the complexity of the task at hand seemed insurmountable. But these challenges only fuelled his desire to learn more. He began to invest in magazines, books, and any resource he could find that would deepen his understanding. His allowance, once reserved for the trivialities of teenage life, was now spent on electronics manuals and parts.

The more Onesimus learned, the more his passion grew. He was no longer the boy lost in the silent corridors of high school; he was a young man on a journey of discovery. His days were filled with trials and triumphs as he navigated through the complexities of his self-imposed curriculum. He wasn't just fixing electronics; he was building a foundation for his future.

As Onesimus's skills improved, so did his confidence. The solitude that had once defined him was now his greatest strength. It had given him the space to grow, to think, and to transform his curiosity into real-world skills. In this quiet space of learning and exploration, Onesimus found his calling.

"Solitude and the Birth of Curiosity" marks a pivotal chapter in Onesimus's life. It's a testament to the power of self-driven learning and the remarkable ways in which solitude can shape a person's destiny. This chapter sets the stage for the future chapters of his life, where the skills and passions developed in solitude become the tools for his entrepreneurial journey.

THE WORLD OF ELECTRONICS

As Onesimus Malatji transitioned from the silent corridors of high school into the broader world, his fascination with electronics transformed from a solitary interest into a profound passion. This chapter delves into how the world of electronics became a gateway for Onesimus to engage with the world, offering him a language he could speak fluently and a space where he felt truly at home.

Within the confines of his personal space, cluttered with wires, tools, and electronic components, Onesimus found a haven. Each piece of equipment he worked on was not just a machine to be fixed; it was a puzzle to be solved, a story to be understood. His self-taught journey took a more serious turn as he delved deeper into the heart of electronics, learning about circuits, programming, and the emerging world of computer technology.

This chapter illuminates Onesimus's growing proficiency in understanding and manipulating electronic devices. His initial trial-and-error methods evolved into more sophisticated techniques. He began to see patterns in the problems he encountered, developing a keen eye for diagnosing and fixing complex issues. The more he learned, the more he realized how vast the field of electronics was, and this realization didn't intimidate him; it invigorated him.

Onesimus's exploration of electronics was more than just a technical pursuit; it was a creative and intellectual journey. He began experimenting with building his own devices, applying the principles he learned to create new projects. These weren't just technical achievements; they were expressions of his creativity, tangible results of his hours of study and experimentation.

The narrative also touches upon the moments of solitude in Onesimus's journey. These were times of reflection, where he contemplated not just the complexities of electronics but also his place in the world. These solitary moments were crucial, as they allowed him to process his learning and apply it in innovative ways.

In "The World of Electronics," we see how Onesimus's passion for electronics provided him with a sense of purpose and direction. It was in this world that he found a sense of belonging and a glimpse of his future potential. This chapter sets the foundation for Onesimus's future endeavours, portraying how his mastery of electronics became the cornerstone of his later success in business and technology. It's a chapter about the transformative power of passion and the endless possibilities that open up when curiosity meets determination.

DREAMS DEFERRED: COLLEGE CHALLENGES

As Onesimus Malatji stepped out of the familiar confines of high school, he entered a new phase of life filled with expectations and aspirations. College was supposed to be the next logical step, a gateway to a promising future. However, for Onesimus, this journey was far from straightforward. This chapter, "Dreams Deferred: College Challenges," delves into the turbulent period of his life when the pursuit of formal education became a series of obstacles, leading to moments of self-doubt and re-evaluation.

Onesimus's entry into college was marked by a sense of hope and anticipation. Driven by his mother's advice and societal expectations, he initially enrolled in mechanical engineering. This decision, however, soon revealed itself to be misaligned with his passions. The rigorous, theory-heavy coursework of engineering felt disconnected from the hands-on, explorative learning he loved in electronics. Struggling to find relevance and joy in his studies, Onesimus's performance began to wane, leading to a growing sense of alienation and frustration.

This chapter poignantly captures the inner turmoil Onesimus experienced during this time. It highlights the struggle of a young man torn between the expectations of his family and society and his own aspirations. The pressure to succeed in a field that didn't resonate with him weighed heavily, leading to a gradual decline in his academic performance and, eventually, to failing his courses.

In a bid to realign with his interests, Onesimus shifted to studying information technology, a field closer to his passion for electronics and computers. However, this change wasn't the solution he had hoped for. The distance-learning format of the IT course, devoid of the interactive and practical elements he thrived on, left him disengaged and unmotivated. His enthusiasm for learning, so evident in his self-taught endeavours, was stifled by the isolating and abstract nature of the curriculum.

The culmination of these experiences led to a pivotal moment in Onesimus's life – the decision to drop out of college. This was not a decision taken lightly; it was a profound moment of realization that the traditional path of education was not his to walk. The chapter explores the emotional and psychological impact of this decision, not just on Onesimus but also on his family. The sense of failure and disappointment was palpable, yet within this setback lay the seeds of future success.

"Dreams Deferred: College Challenges" is a crucial chapter in Onesimus's story. It is about confronting and coming to terms with one's true calling, even when it means going against the grain. This chapter sets the stage for Onesimus's journey towards embracing his true passion, paving the way for his eventual ventures into the world of technology and entrepreneurship.

It's a testament to the idea that sometimes, the path to self-discovery involves navigating through the maze of expectations and finding one's own way, even if it means deferring some dreams along the way.

THE UNFULFILLED PATH OF MECHANICAL ENGINEERING

"The Unfulfilled Path of Mechanical Engineering," delves into a critical phase in Onesimus Malatji's life where his aspirations and reality collided. As he embarked on his journey in mechanical engineering, driven by societal expectations and a desire to fulfil a more traditional academic path, Onesimus found himself in an unfamiliar territory that was misaligned with his true passions.

The chapter opens with Onesimus's initial foray into the world of mechanical engineering. It was a field chosen under the weight of external pressures and expectations rather than his own interest. The course work, with its heavy emphasis on theoretical principles and abstract concepts, was a far cry from the hands-on, explorative nature of electronics that he so deeply loved. Onesimus, who had always found joy in the practical and tangible aspects of learning, struggled to connect with the dry and formulaic approach of engineering studies.

As he delved deeper into his mechanical engineering courses, Onesimus's sense of misalignment grew. The classrooms and lecture halls, filled with equations and theoretical constructs, felt increasingly alien to him. His performance began to reflect his lack of engagement and interest. The grades, once a source of pride in his earlier educational pursuits, now told a story of struggle and disconnect.

This chapter poignantly captures Onesimus's internal conflict during this period. On one hand, there was a desire to succeed and meet the expectations of his family and society. On the other, there was a growing realization that his passion lay elsewhere. The more he engaged with the coursework, the clearer it became that his heart was not in it. This realization led to moments of doubt, frustration, and a questioning of his path.

The narrative takes the reader through the emotional journey of Onesimus as he grapples with the decision of whether to continue on a path that clearly did not resonate with him. This period was marked by introspection, as he began to ponder what truly mattered to him and where his interests genuinely lay.

"The Unfulfilled Path of Mechanical Engineering" is a chapter about coming to terms with one's true self. It highlights the importance of aligning one's career path with personal passions and interests, even when it goes against conventional expectations. For Onesimus, this was a period of learning and growth, albeit in a direction he had not anticipated. It set the stage for his eventual departure from the traditional academic world, steering him towards a journey that was more in tune with his innate interests and talents.

TURNING TO INFORMATION TECHNOLOGY

"Turning to Information Technology," marks a pivotal shift in Onesimus Malatji's educational and personal journey. After the disillusionment he faced in mechanical engineering, Onesimus steered towards a field he believed was more in line with his interests: Information Technology (IT). This chapter explores his transition into IT, the challenges and realizations that came with it, and how this experience further shaped his understanding of his true calling.

The initial switch to IT came with a renewed sense of hope for Onesimus. Here was a field that seemed closer to his passion for electronics and computers, a domain where he could potentially apply his self-taught skills and knowledge. The prospect of studying IT kindled a spark of enthusiasm, a contrast to the dreariness he experienced in mechanical engineering.

However, this newfound enthusiasm soon faced hurdles. The IT course Onesimus enrolled in was a distance-learning program, which, while offering flexibility, lacked the interactive and hands-on learning environment he thrived in. The chapters of textbooks and online materials, though rich in content, could not replicate the tactile and engaging experience of working with actual electronic components and devices. Onesimus found himself grappling with a sense of isolation, reminiscent of his high school days but in a different context.

As the course progressed, Onesimus's initial excitement waned. The solitary nature of distance learning, combined with the abstract and sometimes redundant theoretical aspects of the coursework, left him feeling disengaged and unmotivated. The passion for learning, so evident when he was tinkering with electronics or solving real-world technical problems, seemed to dissipate in the face of uninspiring course modules.

This chapter delves into the internal conflict Onesimus faced during this period. On the one hand, he was aware of the potential opportunities that a formal IT education could offer. On the other, he struggled with the delivery and format of the course, which did not align with his learning style and interests. This disconnect led to a gradual realization that perhaps the traditional educational system, regardless of the field, was not conducive to his personal and professional growth.

"Turning to Information Technology" is a significant chapter in Onesimus's story. It illustrates the challenges of finding the right educational path, the importance of aligning one's learning style with the chosen field of study, and the realization that sometimes, institutional education may not be the answer for everyone. For Onesimus, this experience was another step in his journey towards understanding where his true passion and skills lay, setting the stage for his eventual departure from formal education and a deeper dive into the practical world of technology and entrepreneurship.

THE DROPOUT: A NEW BEGINNING

The decision to leave the world of formal education marked a profound shift in Onesimus Malatji's life. It was a moment filled not with defeat but with the promise of a fresh start, a path that diverged from the well-trodden road of traditional academia. This choice, while daunting in the face of societal expectations and familial pressures, opened a door to a world where Onesimus's true passions could flourish.

Freed from the constraints of a curriculum that never quite aligned with his interests, Onesimus found himself at the crossroads of uncertainty and opportunity. The label of 'dropout' carried a heavy stigma, a societal branding that he now had to navigate. It was a label that brought concern from his family, who had envisioned a different, more conventional academic and professional journey for him.

In the wake of this pivotal decision, Onesimus embarked on a period of deep self-exploration and realignment. The world of textbooks and lecture halls was replaced with a more hands-on, self-directed learning environment. His previous forays into electronics and IT, once relegated to the status of a hobby or a secondary interest, now took centre stage in his life.

This phase was marked by an intense period of learning and experimentation. Onesimus delved deeper into the practical aspects of technology, exploring and expanding his knowledge base beyond the boundaries of traditional education. He began to apply his skills in more concrete ways, discovering the real-world applications of his self-taught expertise.

For Onesimus, this period was more than just about acquiring technical skills; it was about rediscovering his passion and redefining his path. He started to see the potential for a career built not on the expectations of others, but on his own talents and interests. The journey was not without its challenges, as he had to navigate the complexities of building a new life outside the conventional framework of success.

"The Dropout: A New Beginning" is a testament to the power of following one's own path, even when it diverges from societal norms. It highlights the courage required to pursue one's true calling and the resilience needed to forge a new identity beyond the labels imposed by others. For Onesimus, dropping out of college was not the end of his educational journey; it was a bold step into a future where his passions could take flight.

THE OLD 486DX4: A BLESSING IN DISGUISE

Onesimus Malatji's encounter with an old 486DX4 computer, at a time when more advanced models were already on the market, turned out to be a pivotal moment in his journey. This antiquated machine, which initially seemed like a symbol of his family's limited means and his own outdated skills, soon revealed itself to be a hidden treasure, a catalyst for learning and innovation.

The 486DX4, with its limited capabilities and outdated Windows 3.1 operating system, was a far cry from the Pentium 1 models with Windows 95 that his peers boasted. At first, this gap was a source of frustration and embarrassment for Onesimus, especially when his attempts to upgrade or repair the machine led to mockery from those around him. But as he began to work on the computer, his perspective shifted.

Faced with the challenges of repairing and optimizing this older technology, Onesimus found himself delving deeper into the world of computing than ever before. The limitations of the 486DX4 forced him to be creative, to think outside the box, and to explore every nook and cranny of the system's capabilities. It was a process that honed his problem-solving skills, teaching him not just about specific hardware and software, but about patience, persistence, and ingenuity.

The process of fixing and upgrading the 486DX4 became a journey of discovery. Onesimus learned about the intricacies of DOS commands, the nuances of system optimization, and the satisfaction of breathing new life into old technology. Each successful modification was a triumph, a testament to his growing expertise and a step towards realizing his potential in the field of technology.

This chapter, "The Old 486DX4: A Blessing in Disguise," is a reminder that sometimes, the most unassuming and humble beginnings can lead to the greatest learning experiences. For Onesimus, what seemed like a setback became a powerful tool in his journey, helping him to develop the skills and confidence that would shape his future endeavours. This old computer, rather than symbolizing what he lacked, became a profound symbol of his resourcefulness and his ability to turn challenges into opportunities.

FACING MOCKERY AND DOUBT

In his journey, Onesimus Malatji faced not only the technical challenges of working with outdated technology but also the social hurdles of mockery and doubt from those around him. This part of his story delves into how he navigated the scepticism and ridicule that often accompanied his endeavours, particularly when he was seen struggling with his old 486DX4 computer.

The mockery came in various forms – from peers who sneered at the antiquated technology he worked with, to individuals in the tech repair shops who questioned why he bothered with such an outdated machine. These moments were trying for Onesimus, testing his resolve and often making him question his own path. The doubt wasn't just external; it seeped into his own thoughts, challenging his confidence and determination.

Despite these challenges, Onesimus's response to the mockery and doubt was not to retreat but to persist. Each jibe, each sceptical remark, instead of deterring him, became a fuel for his determination. He began to see these challenges as part of his journey, obstacles to be overcome on the way to achieving his goals. This period was instrumental in building his resilience, a quality that would prove invaluable in his later entrepreneurial ventures.

This chapter also touches on the internal struggle that Onesimus faced. Wrestling with self-doubt, he often had to remind himself of the value of his work and his passion for technology. It was a battle between his inner convictions and the external voices of scepticism. Through this struggle, Onesimus learned an important lesson about the nature of innovation and progress – that often, it is misunderstood and undervalued by those who see only the present, not the potential of the future.

"Facing Mockery and Doubt" is a crucial chapter in Onesimus's story. It highlights the emotional and psychological aspects of pursuing a path less travelled. It's a testament to Onesimus's strength of character, showing how he transformed criticism into motivation and scepticism into a challenge to be met. This chapter is about the journey of an innovator who, despite facing doubt from the world around him, continued to believe in himself and his vision.

SELF-EDUCATION: A JOURNEY BEGINS

Embarking on a path less travelled, Onesimus Malatji's journey of self-education became a defining phase in his life. Without the traditional structures of a classroom or the guidance of a formal curriculum, he ventured into a world of learning dictated solely by his curiosity and passion for technology. This chapter explores the genesis and evolution of his self-directed educational journey, highlighting the challenges, triumphs, and transformational experiences along the way.

In the confines of his own space, surrounded by his trusty old 486DX4 and a growing collection of electronics literatures, Onesimus embarked on an unconventional educational path. The absence of a teacher or a structured course did not deter him; instead, it gave him the freedom to explore subjects and topics that genuinely interested him. He delved into the intricate workings of computers, software programming, and the latest technological advancements, driven by an insatiable desire to learn and understand.

This self-guided exploration was not without its trials. Onesimus often encountered complex technical concepts that were difficult to grasp. Without a mentor to turn to, he relied on trial and error, learning from each mistake and misstep. The process was slow and sometimes frustrating, but every challenge he overcame was a victory, a step closer to mastering the skills he sought to acquire.

One of the highlights of this chapter is how Onesimus's self-education extended beyond just technical knowledge. He learned valuable life skills such as problem-solving, critical thinking, and resourcefulness. The discipline and perseverance required to teach oneself were skills that would serve him well in all areas of his life.

"Self-Education: A Journey Begins" is a celebration of the power of self-driven learning. It showcases how Onesimus, armed with determination and a love for technology, created his own educational path. This chapter is a testament to the idea that education is not confined to the walls of a classroom, but can be a lifelong journey fuelled by passion and curiosity. For Onesimus, this journey was not just about acquiring knowledge; it was about shaping his own identity and future.

THE POWER OF DOS

In the midst of his self-education journey, Onesimus Malatji encountered an aspect of computing that would significantly impact his understanding and capabilities: the Disk Operating System, commonly known as DOS. This chapter delves into how Onesimus, armed with his old 486DX4 computer, discovered the power and complexity of DOS, a fundamental component of early computing systems.

Onesimus's journey into the world of DOS began out of necessity. The limitations of his aging computer meant that understanding and mastering DOS was crucial for optimizing its performance. He quickly realized that DOS, with its command-line interface, was not just a tool but a gateway to a deeper understanding of how computers work.

The narrative illustrates Onesimus's initial struggles with the unfamiliar and often intimidating DOS commands. Without the user-friendly graphical interface of modern operating systems, every task in DOS required specific commands and a clear understanding of their functions. Onesimus dedicated countless hours to learning these commands, often experiencing frustration when a particular command did not produce the desired outcome.

However, with persistence, these challenges transformed into triumphs. Each new command he mastered, each problem he solved, was a step forward in his journey.

He began to appreciate the efficiency and control that DOS provided, understanding that this seemingly archaic system laid the groundwork for modern computing.

This chapter also highlights a pivotal moment for Onesimus: the realization of the power of self-reliance in learning. Through his exploration of DOS, he developed a methodical approach to problem-solving, a skill that proved invaluable in his later professional endeavours. He learned not just to follow instructions, but to experiment, deduce, and innovate.

"The Power of DOS" is a significant chapter in Onesimus's story, symbolizing the transition from a novice to someone capable of navigating complex computing environments. It reflects the broader theme of his journey — that perseverance and a willingness to tackle difficult challenges can lead to unexpected growth and empowerment. For Onesimus, DOS was more than just a tool; it was a testament to his ability to adapt, learn, and conquer the challenges that lay on his path to becoming a tech expert.

MEETING AMOS: A NEW MENTOR

As Onesimus Malatji's journey into the depths of technology continued, a chance encounter introduced him to a figure who would significantly influence his path: Amos, a skilled computer technician from Congo. This chapter, "Meeting Amos: A New Mentor," explores the impact of this pivotal meeting on Onesimus's life, marking a transition from solitary exploration to guided learning under the mentorship of an experienced professional.

Amos entered Onesimus's life at a time when he was deeply immersed in self-education, particularly in mastering the nuances of DOS and computer repair. Working for a local computer repair shop, Amos was a brilliant mind in the world of computing, known for his expertise and problem-solving abilities. When Onesimus first brought his old 486DX4 to the shop, he did not anticipate the profound impact this encounter would have on his life.

The narrative delves into the initial interactions between Onesimus and Amos. Despite their different backgrounds, a shared passion for technology quickly formed a bond between them. Amos saw potential in Onesimus's eagerness to learn and offered to mentor him, recognizing a kindred spirit in the young, self-taught enthusiast.

Under Amos's guidance, Onesimus's understanding of computers deepened significantly. Amos introduced him to advanced repair techniques, more complex software issues, and even the business aspects of running a repair service. This mentorship was not confined to technical skills alone; Amos also imparted lessons on professionalism, customer service, and the importance of continuous learning in the ever-evolving field of technology.

For Onesimus, meeting Amos was a transformative experience. It provided him with a broader perspective on the world of computing and technology. The knowledge and skills he acquired under Amos's mentorship complemented his self-taught expertise, creating a well-rounded foundation for his future endeavours.

"Meeting Amos: A New Mentor" is a chapter about the importance of mentorship and the value of learning from those with more experience. It highlights how a mentor can not only impart knowledge but also inspire, challenge, and open new doors for personal and professional growth. For Onesimus, Amos was more than a mentor; he was a catalyst who helped to shape his journey in technology, leaving an indelible mark on his life and career.

THE STRUGGLE WITH COMMANDS

In Onesimus Malatji's journey through the world of computing, his foray into the complexities of DOS commands was a period marked by both frustration and enlightenment. "The Struggle with Commands" delves into this challenging phase, highlighting how the intricacies of DOS became both a hurdle and a crucial learning experience in Onesimus's self-taught path in technology.

For Onesimus, the command-line interface of DOS was a stark departure from the more intuitive graphical user interfaces he was accustomed to. Each command in DOS required precise syntax and a clear understanding of its function. The initial experience was daunting – a single incorrect command could lead to unexpected errors or system crashes, turning the learning process into a trial by fire.

Despite these challenges, Onesimus was determined to master DOS. He spent countless hours poring over manuals and experimenting with different commands, often encountering frustrating setbacks. These moments of struggle were not just about learning the technical aspects of DOS but also about developing perseverance and problem-solving skills. Every error and every system crash, though disheartening, was an opportunity to learn something new.

The narrative in this chapter vividly portrays the ups and downs of Onesimus's journey with DOS. It was a period of self-doubt, where the sheer complexity of commands often made him question his ability to master them. However, these doubts were gradually replaced with a sense of accomplishment as he began to understand and successfully implement the commands.

One of the key aspects of this chapter is how it illustrates the process of learning as an iterative and often challenging journey. Onesimus's struggle with DOS commands is symbolic of the broader learning process in any complex field. It's about the persistence to continue despite difficulties and the resilience to learn from mistakes.

"The Struggle with Commands" is a testament to the fact that true understanding often comes from facing and overcoming challenges. For Onesimus, the struggle with DOS commands was a critical phase in his development as a technologist. It was during this time that he not only developed a strong foundation in computing but also cultivated the tenacity and determination that would define his approach to future challenges in his career.

A DREAM'S COMMAND: THE TURNING POINT

In "A Dream's Command: The Turning Point," Onesimus Malatji's journey through the intricate world of computing takes a surreal and transformative turn. This chapter recounts a remarkable incident where a solution to a persistent technical problem came to Onesimus not through conventional learning, but through a dream — an experience that proved to be a significant turning point in his technological odyssey.

Struggling with a particularly stubborn issue on his 486DX4, Onesimus found himself at a dead end. Despite his growing expertise in DOS commands and computer repair, this problem seemed insurmountable, leaving him frustrated and drained. It was during these times of intense challenge that he experienced something extraordinary.

One night, after hours of fruitless troubleshooting, an exhausted Onesimus drifted into sleep. In his dream, he encountered a vivid and clear instruction: a DOS command sequence that he had not considered. The dream was so real and the instructions so precise that upon waking, Onesimus immediately turned to his computer to try them out. To his astonishment, the commands from his dream resolved the issue perfectly.

This surreal experience was more than just a lucky guess; it was a manifestation of his subconscious mind processing and solving a problem that his conscious mind could not. It was a testament to the depth of his immersion in the world of computing and how his dedication had permeated even his subconscious.

For Onesimus, this event was a revelation. It underscored the power of the human mind to find solutions in the most unexpected ways and at the most unexpected times. It also marked a significant shift in his approach to problem-solving. He began to trust his instincts more, allowing his intuition to guide him through complex technical challenges.

"A Dream's Command: The Turning Point" is a pivotal chapter in Onesimus's story. It illustrates a moment where the boundaries between dream and reality blur, where the subconscious becomes an ally in the quest for knowledge and expertise. This experience not only solved a technical problem but also opened Onesimus's mind to the vast potential within him, reinforcing his belief in his abilities and setting the stage for greater achievements in his technological pursuits.

FIXING THE UNFIXABLE

In "Fixing the Unfixable," Onesimus Malatji's journey as a self-taught technologist takes a remarkable turn, showcasing his growing prowess in overcoming seemingly insurmountable technical challenges. This chapter captures a series of moments where Onesimus, fuelled by his newfound confidence and deepening knowledge, tackles and resolves computer issues that others deemed irreparable.

The narrative begins with Onesimus, fresh from the breakthrough experience of his dream-inspired command success, approaching technical problems with a renewed sense of determination and creativity. The once daunting tasks of troubleshooting and repairing began to feel like puzzles he was eager to solve. His reputation started to grow in his community as someone who could fix even the most problematic computers.

Each new challenge that Onesimus faced was a testament to his evolving skill set. He encountered a variety of complex issues, from hardware malfunctions to software glitches that baffled even seasoned technicians. With a blend of methodical analysis, creative thinking, and sheer perseverance, he began to unravel these problems, often devising unconventional solutions that amazed his peers and clients.

This chapter vividly portrays the satisfaction and sense of accomplishment Onesimus felt with each successful repair. These were not just technical victories but personal triumphs that reinforced his belief in his self-taught path. His ability to fix what others deemed unfixable was not just a demonstration of his technical ability but also a reflection of his approach to life's challenges - facing them head-on, with patience and determination.

"Fixing the Unfixable" also delves into how Onesimus's growing expertise began to change the perception of those around him. The mockery and scepticism he once faced gradually turned into respect and admiration. His journey was becoming a source of inspiration for others, showcasing the power of self-belief and the potential of self-directed learning.

This chapter is a crucial part of Onesimus's story, highlighting a period where his skills, honed through years of dedicated self-learning and experimentation, truly began to shine. It's a testament to the idea that with enough dedication and passion, what may seem unfixable can indeed be fixed, a metaphor that extended well beyond the realm of computer repair to the broader challenges of life and career.

MOLEFE: A FRIEND AND COLLABORATOR

In the chapter "Molefe: A Friend and Collaborator," Onesimus Malatji's narrative takes a significant turn as he forges a pivotal relationship with Molefe, a character who emerges as both a friend and a business associate. This encounter marks a transition from solitary learning to collaborative enterprise, expanding Onesimus's horizons in the world of technology and entrepreneurship.

The story unfolds as Onesimus, having established a reputation as a skilled computer technician, crosses paths with Molefe. Molefe, himself a bright mind with a keen interest in software programming, had recently faced his own set of challenges, including dropping out of school due to financial constraints. The initial connection between Onesimus and Molefe was rooted in their shared passion for technology and their similar paths of self-directed learning.

Molefe brought a new dimension to Onesimus's world. His expertise in software complemented Onesimus's hardware proficiency, creating a synergy that was both dynamic and fruitful. As they began to collaborate, their combined skills opened up new opportunities. They started working on small projects together, gradually taking on more complex tasks and even considering entrepreneurial ventures.

This chapter explores the evolution of their partnership. From fixing computers and developing software solutions, they began to dream bigger. Their discussions started to revolve around starting a joint venture, combining their skills to offer a more comprehensive range of tech services. This period was marked by brainstorming sessions, planning, and the excitement of potential business prospects.

"Molefe: A Friend and Collaborator" delves into the dynamics of their relationship, highlighting the importance of partnership in business. It shows how collaboration can bring out the best in each individual, leading to growth and development that might not be possible alone. For Onesimus, meeting Molefe wasn't just about finding a business partner; it was about building a relationship that would challenge him, push him to think bigger, and ultimately help him grow both professionally and personally.

This chapter is a celebration of friendship, collaboration, and the shared journey of two like-minded individuals. It underscores the value of connecting with others who share similar passions and aspirations, and how such connections can lead to fruitful and fulfilling endeavours. For Onesimus and Molefe, their partnership was more than just a business arrangement; it was a union of minds and talents that set the foundation for future successes.

THE BIRTH OF A BUSINESS PARTNERSHIP

In "The Birth of a Business Partnership," the narrative of Onesimus Malatji's life takes a decisive turn towards entrepreneurship. This chapter details the formation of a business partnership between Onesimus and Molefe, marking a significant transition from individual pursuits to a collective venture. It captures the excitement, challenges, and potential of their joint endeavour in the world of technology.

As their collaboration deepened, Onesimus and Molefe recognized the potential in combining their respective strengths. Onesimus, with his expertise in hardware and troubleshooting, complemented Molefe's skills in software development and programming. The realization that they could offer a more comprehensive service by working together led to the decision to formalize their partnership.

The formation of their business was not without challenges. They had to navigate the intricacies of starting and running a business, from legalities and financial planning to marketing and client acquisition. This part of their journey involved learning new skills beyond their technical expertise, such as understanding market needs, managing finances, and developing a business strategy.

The narrative highlights the initial steps they took to establish their venture. This included defining their business model, setting up a workspace, and identifying their target market.

They pooled their resources, combining Onesimus's hands-on technical knowledge with Molefe's programming acumen, to create a unique offering in the local tech landscape.

The excitement of starting their own business was palpable. Onesimus and Molefe spent countless hours planning, discussing potential projects, and brainstorming ways to innovate and stand out in a competitive market. The chapter captures the optimism and energy of this phase, as well as the sense of accomplishment in seeing their shared vision take shape.

"The Birth of a Business Partnership" is a crucial chapter in Onesimus's story. It represents a significant leap in his professional life, moving from a self-taught individual to a co-founder of a business. This chapter is about the power of collaboration, the importance of complementing skills, and the transformative journey from idea to reality in the entrepreneurial world. For Onesimus and Molefe, this partnership was a bold step into a future filled with possibilities, challenges, and the promise of success.

THE FIRST BIG PROJECT

In "The First Big Project," Onesimus Malatji and Molefe, emboldened by their new partnership, embark on their inaugural venture. This chapter chronicles their first significant undertaking, a venture that not only tested their combined skills and resolve but also set the tone for their future business endeavours.

The project came as an opportunity to provide comprehensive tech solutions for a local school named Tswelelang. The task was daunting yet exhilarating: they were to supply, set up, and maintain twenty computers for the school's new computer lab. This project was not just a business opportunity; it was a chance to make a tangible impact in their community and to lay the groundwork for their reputation as a reliable tech service provider.

Onesimus and Molefe approached this project with a blend of excitement and seriousness. They recognized that the success of this project could open doors for future business and establish their credibility in the market. The planning phase was meticulous. Onesimus's expertise in hardware was crucial in selecting the right computers and setting them up, while Molefe's software skills ensured that the systems were optimally configured and user-friendly.

This chapter vividly describes the challenges they faced, from logistical hurdles to meeting the specific needs of the school. They worked tirelessly, often late into the night, troubleshooting problems and ensuring everything was in perfect order. The learning curve was steep; every obstacle they encountered and overcame was a lesson in resilience, teamwork, and the nuances of managing a large-scale project.

The day of the lab's inauguration was a moment of triumph for Onesimus and Molefe. Seeing the lab bustling with students exploring their new computers was a deeply gratifying experience. It was a validation of their skills, their business model, and their vision. The successful completion of this project was more than just a professional achievement; it was a realization of their potential as entrepreneurs.

"The First Big Project" is a pivotal chapter in Onesimus's entrepreneurial journey. It highlights the transition from concept to execution, the challenges of scaling up from small tasks to larger projects, and the satisfaction of seeing one's efforts come to fruition. This project laid the foundation for their business, proving that with the right blend of skills, determination, and teamwork, they could tackle significant challenges and emerge successfully.

RISING TENSIONS: THE SPLIT

As Onesimus Malatji and Molefe navigated the complexities of their burgeoning business, "Rising Tensions: The Split" chronicles a challenging period that tested the strength and sustainability of their partnership. This chapter delves into the underlying issues and conflicts that began to surface, ultimately leading to a significant rift in their collaboration.

The success of their first big project had initially brought a wave of optimism and a sense of accomplishment. However, as their business continued to grow, so did the pressures and demands. Differences in their visions for the future of the company, management styles, and approaches to handling business challenges began to emerge. These differences, initially subtle, started to create a wedge between the two partners.

Onesimus, with his methodical and detail-oriented approach, found himself at odds with Molefe's more aggressive expansion plans and risk-taking strategies. Disagreements over financial management, project priorities, and business development strategies became more frequent. The narrative illustrates how these professional differences were compounded by communication breakdowns and misunderstandings, further straining their relationship.

The chapter paints a picture of the emotional and psychological impact of this period on Onesimus. He grappled with the realization that the partnership, which had started with shared dreams and mutual respect, was now in jeopardy. The sense of camaraderie and teamwork that had driven their early successes was being overshadowed by conflict and discord.

The climax of this chapter is the eventual split between Onesimus and Molefe. This decision, though painful, was the culmination of ongoing tensions and unresolved differences. It marked a turning point in Onesimus's entrepreneurial journey, closing a chapter of collaboration but also opening new avenues for individual growth and exploration.

"Rising Tensions: The Split" is a candid exploration of the challenges inherent in business partnerships. It highlights the importance of aligned visions, effective communication, and mutual understanding in a successful collaboration. For Onesimus, this split was not just an end to a partnership but a learning experience that provided valuable insights into the complexities of running a business and the importance of adaptability and resilience in the face of change.

THE PATH OF TEACHING AND SHARING KNOWLEDGE

After the split with Molefe, Onesimus Malatji embarked on a new phase in his journey: the path of teaching and sharing knowledge. This chapter, "The Path of Teaching and Sharing Knowledge," explores Onesimus's transition from primarily focusing on business ventures to also becoming an educator and mentor in the field of technology.

With the experiences and expertise, he had accumulated, Onesimus recognized a growing need in his community for technological education. He saw an opportunity to not only expand his professional scope but also to give back by imparting his knowledge to others. This shift was driven by a desire to empower those around him with the skills and understanding that had been so transformative in his own life.

Onesimus began by offering informal classes and workshops on basic computer skills, hardware maintenance, and software usage. His teaching style, grounded in his own self-taught journey and practical experience, resonated with his students. He had a unique ability to demystify complex technological concepts, making them accessible and understandable to people with little to no prior experience.

The narrative details how Onesimus's role as an educator quickly grew. What started as small, informal sessions soon expanded into more structured classes.

He began to collaborate with local schools and community centres, developing curriculums that catered to different age groups and skill levels. His classes covered a wide range of topics, from basic computer literacy to more advanced subjects like network setup and cybersecurity.

This chapter also delves into the gratification Onesimus felt in this new role. Teaching and sharing his knowledge became a source of fulfilment, providing a sense of purpose beyond the pursuit of business success. He found joy in witnessing the growth and development of his students, and in the knowledge that he was contributing to the technological empowerment of his community.

"The Path of Teaching and Sharing Knowledge" is a testament to the power of education and mentorship. It illustrates how Onesimus's journey came full circle – from a self-taught learner to a guide and mentor for others. This chapter highlights the impact that sharing knowledge can have, not just on the recipients of that knowledge, but also on the one who shares it. For Onesimus, teaching became an extension of his entrepreneurial spirit, a new avenue through which he could continue to innovate, inspire, and make a difference in the world of technology.

COMPUGEM: A NEW ALLIANCE

Following his foray into teaching and mentoring, Onesimus Malatji encountered a new opportunity that would further expand his impact in the world of technology. In "Compugem: A New Alliance," the narrative shifts to Onesimus's collaboration with Compugem, a local computer school. This chapter illustrates how this partnership not only broadened his professional horizons but also deepened his commitment to technological education in his community.

Compugem, known for its computer literacy programs and vocational training, was an ideal match for Onesimus's expertise and newly discovered passion for teaching. The alliance began with mutual recognition of the potential benefits their collaboration could bring. For Compugem, Onesimus's practical experience and ability to translate complex technological concepts into accessible learning made him an invaluable asset. For Onesimus, the partnership provided a structured platform to reach a wider audience and to formalize his teaching endeavours.

This chapter delves into the development of their collaborative efforts. Onesimus worked closely with Computer's team to develop curriculum and training programs that combined theoretical knowledge with practical, hands-on experience. He became an integral part of the teaching staff, bringing his unique perspective and methods to the classroom.

The alliance with Compugem also marked a period of significant professional growth for Onesimus. He found himself at the forefront of a growing movement to enhance technological literacy, a crucial skill in the increasingly digital global landscape. His work with the school allowed him to influence the curriculum, ensuring that it remained relevant and responsive to the evolving technological environment.

"Compugem: A New Alliance" highlights the successes and challenges of this partnership. While it opened new doors and provided a fulfilling avenue to impart knowledge, it also presented challenges such as aligning different educational philosophies and managing administrative responsibilities.

Through this chapter, Onesimus's story underscores the importance of collaborations in achieving broader goals. His partnership with Compugem was more than a business venture; it was a fusion of shared objectives to empower individuals through education. This alliance not only reinforced Onesimus's role as an educator and mentor but also underscored the value of community-oriented initiatives in the field of technology.

THE BREAKDOWN OF A PARTNERSHIP

The Breakdown of a Partnership" delves into a challenging phase in Onesimus Malatji's professional journey, detailing the unravelling of his collaborative relationship with Compugem. This chapter explores the complexities and nuances of a partnership facing difficulties, highlighting the factors that contributed to its eventual dissolution.

The alliance with Compugem had initially appeared to be a perfect match, blending Onesimus's expertise and passion for teaching with Compugem's established platform and resources. However, as time progressed, cracks began to emerge in this seemingly ideal partnership. Diverging visions for the future of the educational programs, disagreements over management styles, and differing priorities started to strain the relationship.

Onesimus found himself increasingly at odds with Compugem's administrative and operational decisions. Where he envisioned a more hands-on, practical approach to teaching technology, the school management leaned towards a more traditional, theory-heavy curriculum. These differences extended beyond educational philosophies to include disagreements on resource allocation, program development, and student engagement strategies.

The narrative delves into the emotional and professional impact of these tensions on Onesimus. He grappled with the realization that the partnership, which had started with much enthusiasm and shared goals, was now being overshadowed by conflict and disillusionment. The sense of fulfilment he had once found in this collaboration was diminishing, replaced by frustration and a feeling of being constrained.

The climax of this chapter is the decision to part ways with Compugem. This decision, though difficult, was the culmination of ongoing unresolved issues and divergent paths. It marked a turning point for Onesimus, prompting him to re-evaluate his goals and approach to his work in technology and education.

"The Breakdown of a Partnership" is a candid exploration of the challenges inherent in collaborative ventures. It underscores the importance of aligned visions, effective communication, and mutual understanding in a successful partnership. For Onesimus, this experience, while disheartening, provided valuable lessons in the complexities of professional relationships and the importance of staying true to one's principles and vision. The end of his partnership with Compugem, though a setback, set the stage for new beginnings and opportunities, reinforcing his resilience and adaptability in the face of change.

LOXION ONYS PRINTING AGENCY: THE START

After the dissolution of his partnership with Compugem, Onesimus Malatji embarked on a new venture, marking another significant chapter in his journey. "Loxion Onys Printing Agency: The Start" chronicles the establishment of his own business, a venture that would not only harness his technological skills but also reflect his entrepreneurial spirit.

Onesimus's decision to start Loxion Onys Printing Agency stemmed from a desire to combine his love for technology with a service that was in high demand within his community. Recognizing the growing need for printing services – from business cards and flyers to educational materials – he saw an opportunity to fill a niche in the local market.

This chapter details the initial stages of setting up the business. Onesimus, drawing upon his experiences and lessons learned from previous ventures, began the process with a clear vision. He invested in quality printing equipment, leveraging his technical expertise to maintain and optimize the machines. His approach was to offer not just printing services, but solutions tailored to the specific needs of his clients, ensuring quality and affordability.

The narrative explores the challenges and triumphs of these early days. Starting a business from scratch involved more than just technical know-how; it required marketing, customer relations, and financial management. Onesimus navigated these challenges with a hands-on approach, gradually building a client base through word-of-mouth and community engagement.

"Loxion Onys Printing Agency: The Start" also delves into how Onesimus's venture quickly became more than just a business. It was a platform for community engagement and empowerment. He offered training sessions on basic graphic design and printing, sharing his knowledge and skills with local youths and entrepreneurs. This aspect of the business added another layer of fulfilment to his work, aligning with his deep-seated values of education and community service.

The establishment of Loxion Onys Printing Agency represents a pivotal moment in Onesimus's story, illustrating his resilience and adaptability. It was a venture that combined his technical acumen with his entrepreneurial ambitions, setting a new path in his career. This chapter is a testament to the power of perseverance, the importance of adapting to change, and the potential to create opportunities even in the face of challenges.

ENTERING THE WORLD OF GRAPHIC DESIGN

As Onesimus Malatji's Loxion Onys Printing Agency began to find its footing, a new dimension was added to his entrepreneurial journey: the world of graphic design. "Entering the World of Graphic Design" charts Onesimus's foray into this creative field, a move that not only expanded the services of his business but also opened a new avenue for personal and professional growth.

Initially, the printing agency primarily focused on basic printing services. However, as Onesimus interacted with clients, he recognized a growing demand for custom design work. Clients frequently requested designs for the materials they wanted to print, from simple business cards to more complex promotional materials. Seeing this as an opportunity to enhance his business offerings, Onesimus decided to delve into the realm of graphic design.

This chapter vividly depicts Onesimus's initial plunge into graphic design. With little formal training in the field, he relied on his self-taught ethos and began to learn the necessary skills. He invested in design software, pored over online tutorials, and experimented with various design tools. The learning curve was steep, but Onesimus's determination and adaptability shone through as he gradually mastered the basics of graphic design.

The narrative explores the challenges Onesimus faced in this new endeavour. Graphic design required not only technical skills but also a creative eye and an understanding of client needs. Onesimus worked tirelessly to refine his design skills, often spending late nights experimenting with different layouts, colour schemes, and typography.

As his proficiency grew, so did the reputation of Loxion Onys Printing Agency as a one-stop shop for both printing and design needs. Onesimus started to take on more complex design projects, eventually building a portfolio that attracted a wider range of clients. His journey into graphic design became a significant aspect of his business, setting it apart from competitors and allowing for greater creativity and client customization.

"Entering the World of Graphic Design" is a chapter that highlights Onesimus's continuous pursuit of learning and growth. It underscores his ability to identify and seize opportunities, adapting his business to meet market demands. This foray into graphic design not only enhanced his business but also allowed Onesimus to express his creativity and further establish himself as a versatile and resourceful entrepreneur.

A LIE TURNED OPPORTUNITY

In "A Lie Turned Opportunity," Onesimus Malatji's entrepreneurial journey took an unexpected twist when a chance to expand his business hinged on a small but significant untruth. This chapter explores how a moment of improvisation under pressure led to a transformative opportunity, propelling Onesimus deeper into the world of graphic design.

Faced with a client's request for custom graphic design at Loxion Onys Printing Agency, Onesimus found himself at a crossroads. Despite his limited experience in graphic design, he made a split-second decision to affirm his proficiency in Corel Draw, a well-known design software. This assertion, more a reflection of his ambition than his current skill set, set the stage for a crucial period of rapid learning and development.

The narrative details the intense and urgent journey that Onesimus embarked on following this claim. Recognizing the risk of overpromising and underdelivering, he immersed himself in the world of Corel Draw. Night after night, he dedicated himself to mastering the software, exploring its functionalities, and experimenting with design techniques. This period was marked by a mix of fear and excitement – fear of failure and the excitement of venturing into uncharted territory.

Onesimus's commitment to learning under pressure is a central theme of this chapter. His efforts to bridge the gap between his promise and his actual skills exemplify his determination and resilience. Each successful design he created not only built his confidence but also enhanced his reputation as a versatile service provider.

The culmination of this episode was significant for Onesimus. Not only did he deliver on his commitment to the client, but he also unlocked a new potential for his business. Graphic design quickly became an integral part of the services offered by Loxion Onys Printing Agency, adding a new dimension to the business and attracting a broader clientele.

"A Lie Turned Opportunity" is a pivotal chapter in Onesimus's story, highlighting the sometimes-blurred lines between risk and opportunity in entrepreneurship. It underscores the idea that moments of challenge can become catalysts for growth, pushing individuals beyond their comfort zones and into new realms of possibility. For Onesimus, what began as a precarious assertion transformed into a key milestone in his professional development and the expansion of his business.

MASTERING COREL DRAW

"Mastering Corel Draw" delves into a significant chapter in Onesimus Malatji's entrepreneurial journey, where he embarks on the challenge of transforming his tentative claim into a tangible skill. This chapter narrates his dedicated pursuit to master Corel Draw, a journey marked by determination, rapid learning, and the evolution of a new skill set that would significantly enhance his business capabilities.

Initially, Onesimus's interaction with Corel Draw was limited and elementary. However, faced with the need to fulfil the commitment he made to his client, he plunged into an intense period of self-education. This phase of his journey was characterized by long nights spent exploring the software, experimenting with its various tools, and understanding its vast capabilities.

The narrative highlights the challenges Onesimus faced as he navigated through Corel Draw. Each tool and feature presented a new learning curve. He tackled vector graphics, layout designs, colour theory, and typography, slowly building his competence. His approach was methodical and disciplined, reflecting his resolve to not only learn but excel in using the software.

As Onesimus's proficiency with Corel Draw grew, so did his confidence. He started taking on small design projects, applying his newfound skills in practical scenarios.

With each completed project, he not only honed his craft but also started to appreciate the creative aspect of graphic design, a contrast to the more technical work he was accustomed to.

This chapter also explores how Onesimus began to integrate his design services with the printing solutions offered at Loxion Onys Printing Agency. The addition of graphic design services transformed his business, attracting a wider array of clients and projects. Onesimus's ability to offer a complete package from design to print became a unique selling point, setting his business apart in the local market.

"Mastering Corel Draw" is a testament to Onesimus's relentless pursuit of growth and adaptation. It underscores the power of self-directed learning and the importance of continually acquiring new skills in response to market needs. For Onesimus, mastering Corel Draw was not just about adding a service to his business; it was about embracing change, challenging himself, and exploring the convergence of technology and creativity.

THE BUSINESS OF CREATIVITY

In "The Business of Creativity," Onesimus Malatji's narrative transitions into an exploration of how he seamlessly blended his technical prowess with his newly acquired skills in graphic design, thus transforming Loxion Onys Printing Agency into a dynamic enterprise. This chapter delves into the multifaceted role creativity played in his business, highlighting the challenges and opportunities of integrating artistic vision with practical business solutions.

As Onesimus mastered Corel Draw, he began to view graphic design not just as an additional service but as a core element of his business model. This integration marked a significant shift in his professional approach, elevating the role of creativity to be on par with technological proficiency. He started to approach every project as an opportunity to craft something unique and meaningful, going beyond mere functionality to add aesthetic value.

This chapter explores the intricacies of managing a business where creativity is a key component. Onesimus navigated the balance between artistic expression and the practicalities of running a business, such as meeting client expectations, adhering to deadlines, and maintaining profitability. He learned to marry aesthetic appeal with functional design, ensuring that his creations were not only visually striking but also effectively served their intended purpose.

A pivotal aspect of Onesimus's journey highlighted in this chapter is his ability to forge strong relationships with clients through creative collaboration. He adopted a consultative approach to design, involving clients in the creative process to ensure their vision and objectives were accurately reflected in the final product. This personalized approach led to enhanced customer satisfaction, fostering loyalty and generating positive word-of-mouth referrals.

"The Business of Creativity" also reflects on Onesimus's impact within his community. His work transcended typical business transactions; it contributed to the cultural and economic fabric of the local area. Whether designing branding materials for emerging businesses or creating educational resources for schools, his creative contributions had a lasting and positive impact.

For Onesimus, integrating creativity into his business was more than just a strategic decision; it was a journey of personal and professional growth. This chapter not only illustrates the challenges and rewards of running a creative business but also showcases Onesimus's evolution as an entrepreneur. He demonstrated that embracing creativity in technology can lead to a more enriching business experience, driving innovation and distinguishing his enterprise in a competitive market.

SOSHA TIMES AND AFRICA NTSHEBELE

"Sosha Times and Africa Ntshebele" marks a notable chapter in Onesimus Malatji's entrepreneurial story, showcasing his venture into the world of publication. This chapter highlights how Onesimus, leveraging his skills in graphic design and printing, expanded his business into the realm of publishing, thereby marking his entry into a new and challenging industry.

Onesimus identified an opportunity in the local market for community-focused publications. He envisioned 'Sosha Times' and 'Africa Ntshebele' as platforms that would not only provide local news and stories but also celebrate the culture and achievements of his community. This initiative was driven by a desire to give a voice to local narratives and to create publications that resonated with the people in his area.

The creation of 'Sosha Times' and 'Africa Ntshebele' involved more than just printing; it required content curation, layout design, and a keen understanding of the audience. Onesimus drew upon his experiences in graphic design to create visually appealing layouts and used his business acumen to handle the logistics of publishing. He collaborated with local writers and journalists, building a team that could bring authentic and engaging stories to life.

This chapter delves into the challenges Onesimus faced in this new venture. Navigating the publishing industry presented obstacles such as distribution logistics, advertising sales, and maintaining a consistent and high-quality content flow. Onesimus tackled these challenges head-on, applying his problem-solving skills and learning from each new experience.

The launch of 'Sosha Times' and 'Africa Ntshebele' was met with enthusiasm from the community. These publications filled a gap in local media, offering a fresh perspective and coverage that was more aligned with the interests and needs of the local populace. Onesimus's commitment to quality and relevance paid off, as the readership for both publications grew steadily.

"Sosha Times and Africa Ntshebele" is a chapter about innovation, community engagement, and the power of media to connect and inform. It showcases Onesimus's ability to venture into new territories and his dedication to serving his community. These publications were not just business endeavours; they were a reflection of Onesimus's deep-rooted commitment to giving back to his community and contributing positively to the local cultural landscape.

THE BIRTH OF STREET IS WAAR

"The Birth of Street is Waar" chronicles a significant expansion in Onesimus Malatji's entrepreneurial repertoire, marking his foray into a niche yet impactful area of publication. This chapter details the inception, development, and launch of "Street is Waar," a publication that aimed to capture the vibrant street culture and the dynamic urban life of Onesimus's community.

Onesimus conceptualized "Street is Waar" as a platform to showcase local talent, street art, music, fashion, and the everyday stories that define the rhythm of street life. His intention was to create a publication that resonated deeply with the youth and the broader community, offering content that was both relatable and inspirational.

The creation of "Street is Waar" was a venture that combined Onesimus's skills in graphic design and printing with his keen understanding of local culture. He envisioned the publication as not just a business venture but as a cultural artifact – a medium that reflected and celebrated the diversity and creativity of street culture. This project required him to step into the realms of editorial planning, content curation, and creative direction.

This chapter highlights the collaborative process involved in bringing "Street is Waar" to life. Onesimus engaged with local artists, writers, and photographers, creating a collaborative platform that was rich in diversity and creativity. The process was a learning experience, requiring him to balance creative inputs with the practical aspects of publishing a regular magazine.

Launching "Street is Waar" was a bold move in a competitive market. The initial reception was a mix of excitement and curiosity from the community. The magazine's authentic content, coupled with high-quality design and print, quickly garnered a dedicated readership. Onesimus's commitment to capturing the essence of street culture struck a chord with many, establishing "Street is Waar" as a unique and respected voice in the community.

"The Birth of Street is Waar" is a testament to Onesimus's vision and his ability to identify and fill a gap in the market. This chapter illustrates his entrepreneurial agility and his dedication to projects that not only contribute to his business growth but also have a meaningful impact on the community. "Street is Waar" became more than a publication; it was a celebration of the culture and life of the streets, encapsulating the pulse of the community in its pages.

CYBERCAFE: A COMMUNITY HAVEN

In the chapter "Cybercafe: A Community Haven," the narrative of Onesimus Malatji's entrepreneurial journey shifts to a new venture that would not only enhance his business portfolio but also significantly contribute to his community. This chapter explores the inception, development, and impact of Onesimus's cybercafe, a venture that emerged as a vital resource and gathering spot within his community.

Recognizing the growing importance of internet access and digital literacy, Onesimus saw an opportunity to create a space that would provide these essential services. His vision was to establish a cybercafe that would serve as more than just an internet hub; it was to be a community centre where people could connect, learn, and grow in the digital age.

The journey to establish the cybercafe began with identifying a suitable location, acquiring the necessary technology, and setting up a welcoming and functional space. Onesimus invested in quality computers, reliable internet connectivity, and a comfortable setting to ensure that his customers had a positive experience. His background in technology played a crucial role in setting up and maintaining the technical aspects of the cybercafe.

This chapter vividly describes the challenges and triumphs of running the cybercafe. Managing a public internet space came with its unique set of challenges, from ensuring internet safety and security to handling the diverse needs of customers. Onesimus navigated these challenges with a focus on providing quality service and fostering a safe and inclusive environment.

The cybercafe quickly became a community haven. It attracted a diverse clientele, from students who came to research and complete assignments to entrepreneurs who utilized the space for business purposes. Onesimus also offered basic computer training sessions, helping to bridge the digital divide and empowering community members with essential digital skills.

"Cybercafe: A Community Haven" highlights the impact of the cybercafe on the community. It became a place where people could access information, learn new skills, and connect with others in the digital world. The cafe's success extended beyond its commercial achievements; it played a vital role in enhancing digital literacy and accessibility in the community.

For Onesimus, the cybercafe was a reflection of his entrepreneurial spirit and his commitment to social responsibility. This venture demonstrated how a business could serve the dual purpose of being economically viable while also making a significant contribution to the community's well-being and growth. The cybercafe was not just a business venture; it was a testament to Onesimus's vision of leveraging technology to create opportunities and foster community development.

EXPANSION: THE DURBAN ADVENTURE

"Expansion: The Durban Adventure" narrates a bold and ambitious chapter in Onesimus Malatji's entrepreneurial journey. Following the success of his cybercafe in his local community, Onesimus embarked on an expansion of his business model to Durban, a decision that marked a significant leap in his professional life and illustrated his willingness to venture into new territories.

Driven by the success of the cybercafe as a community hub and a centre for digital access and learning, Onesimus recognized the potential for replicating this model in other regions. Durban, with its vibrant urban landscape and diverse population, presented an exciting opportunity for expansion. This decision was fuelled by both the desire to grow his business and to replicate the positive community impact he had achieved in his hometown.

The narrative details the planning and execution of this expansion. Onesimus conducted thorough market research, assessing the needs and dynamics of the Durban community to tailor his cybercafe model accordingly. He faced the logistical challenges of setting up a business in a new city, from finding the right location to establishing a supply chain for equipment and services.

Onesimus's venture into Durban was a journey filled with challenges and learning experiences. He navigated new regulatory environments, different customer expectations, and the task of building a customer base from scratch. Despite these hurdles, his commitment to providing quality service and fostering a community-focused environment remained steadfast.

The chapter also highlights the importance of adaptability in business. Onesimus had to make several adjustments to his original cybercafe model to suit the unique characteristics and needs of the Durban community. This process of adaptation was crucial in ensuring the relevance and success of the new cybercafe.

"Expansion: The Durban Adventure" is a testament to Onesimus's entrepreneurial spirit and his ability to scale his business. The successful establishment of the cybercafe in Durban not only marked a significant milestone in his business career but also reinforced his vision of using technology to empower communities. This expansion venture was more than just a business growth strategy; it was an embodiment of Onesimus's dedication to making technology accessible and beneficial to a broader audience.

THE SPLIT OF ONY LE EDY

"The Split of ONY LE EDY" delves into a pivotal yet challenging moment in Onesimus Malatji's business journey. This chapter explores the circumstances and events leading to the dissolution of ONY LE EDY, a joint venture that Onesimus had embarked on with his brother, Edy. The split signifies a crucial turning point, highlighting the complexities of family-run businesses and the difficult decisions that sometimes have to be made for individual and collective growth.

Onesimus and Edy had initially come together with a shared vision, combining their strengths and resources to expand the reach and impact of their cybercafe business. ONY LE EDY, representing a fusion of their names and aspirations, had successfully established itself in both their hometown and Durban, becoming a symbol of their collaborative success.

However, as the business grew, differences in their visions and management styles began to surface. Onesimus, with his keen focus on community impact and technological empowerment, often found himself at odds with Edy's more profit-driven approach. These differing philosophies, compounded by the everyday pressures of running a growing enterprise, began to strain their partnership.

This chapter outlines the emotional and professional challenges that both brothers faced as they navigated this period of tension. The decision to part ways was not arrived at lightly. It involved intense discussions, reflections on their individual goals, and considerations of the future of ONY LE EDY. The split, while amicable, was a complex process, involving the division of assets, responsibilities, and future directions.

For Onesimus, "The Split of ONY LE EDY" was more than just the end of a business partnership; it was a moment of profound personal and professional introspection. It forced him to reassess his goals, strategies, and the path he wanted to forge moving forward. This chapter also touches upon the resilience and adaptability required to navigate such a significant change, especially when it involves family.

The dissolution of ONY LE EDY marked the beginning of a new chapter for Onesimus. It was a period of realignment and renewed focus on his entrepreneurial journey. This chapter showcases the evolution of a business and its founders, underscoring the notion that sometimes, moving forward requires making tough decisions, even if it means walking separate paths.

CYBER INFLUX: A NEW IDENTITY

"Cyber Influx: A New Identity" marks a transformative chapter in Onesimus Malatji's entrepreneurial journey. Following the split of ONY LE EDY, Onesimus embarked on rebranding and reshaping his business, leading to the birth of 'Cyber Influx.' This chapter narrates how Onesimus, navigating through the aftermath of the split, reinvented his cybercafe venture, infusing it with new energy and direction.

Post the split, Onesimus was faced with the challenge of redefining his business and his role within the community. He envisioned 'Cyber Influx' as not just a continuation of his previous venture but as a reimagined space that reflected his evolving business philosophy and the changing needs of his customers.

The narrative details the rebranding process, highlighting the strategic decisions involved in creating a new identity for the cybercafe. 'Cyber Influx' was conceptualized to be more than a place for internet access; it was designed to be a hub for technology, learning, and community interaction. Onesimus invested in upgrading the technology and infrastructure, ensuring that 'Cyber Influx' offered a superior experience to its users.

This chapter also delves into the innovative additions Onesimus introduced at 'Cyber Influx.' He expanded the range of services to include more advanced digital services like web design, digital marketing, and tech consultancy. Recognizing the importance of digital literacy, he also intensified his focus on educational workshops and training programs, aiming to empower his community with the skills needed in a digital world.

Onesimus's journey with 'Cyber Influx' was not without its challenges. The rebranding process required not only financial investment but also a significant effort in marketing and customer engagement to establish the new brand. Onesimus navigated these challenges with a mix of creative strategies and sheer determination.

"Cyber Influx: A New Identity" is a story of resilience and innovation. It showcases how Onesimus transformed a period of change and uncertainty into an opportunity for growth and reinvention. This chapter reflects the dynamic nature of entrepreneurship – the need to continuously adapt, evolve, and stay attuned to the shifting landscapes of business and technology. 'Cyber Influx' became a testament to Onesimus's commitment to his business ideals and his dedication to serving his community through technology.

ENTERING TELECOMMUNICATIONS

"Entering Telecommunications" is a pivotal chapter in Onesimus Malatji's entrepreneurial saga, marking his venture into the complex and rapidly evolving telecommunications sector. This move represented a significant leap from his previous endeavours, showcasing his ambition to not only adapt to technological advancements but also to play an active role in shaping them.

Following the successful rebranding of 'Cyber Influx,' Onesimus recognized the burgeoning potential in the telecommunications industry. He saw an opportunity to diversify his business and address a growing need in his community for better connectivity and telecommunication services.

This chapter details Onesimus's journey into the telecommunications world, a path laden with both opportunities and challenges. He began by conducting extensive research into the industry, understanding the technological requirements, market trends, and regulatory frameworks. His foray into this field required substantial investment in both time and resources, as well as navigating the complexities of a highly regulated industry.

One of the key elements of this venture was establishing partnerships with existing telecommunications providers. Onesimus leveraged these partnerships to bring enhanced internet and communication services to his community. His goal was to provide affordable and reliable connectivity, bridging the digital divide and opening up new possibilities for local residents and businesses.

The narrative also explores the challenges that Onesimus faced in this new venture. Entering a highly competitive industry posed significant hurdles, from acquiring the necessary technical expertise to competing with established players in the market. Onesimus tackled these challenges head-on, utilizing his entrepreneurial acumen to carve out a niche for 'Cyber Influx' in the telecommunications landscape.

"Entering Telecommunications" is a testament to Onesimus's relentless pursuit of growth and his ability to identify and capitalize on new business opportunities. This chapter illustrates his journey of transforming 'Cyber Influx' from a local cybercafe into a multifaceted enterprise, underscoring his vision to continually evolve and stay ahead in the fast-paced world of technology. The move into telecommunications not only expanded the scope of his business operations but also reinforced his commitment to empowering his community through technological advancement.

THE CHALLENGE OF REMOTE CONNECTIVITY

In the chapter "The Challenge of Remote Connectivity," Onesimus Malatji's venture into the telecommunications sector encounters a significant hurdle – the task of providing reliable internet connectivity in remote and underserved areas. This challenge underscores the complexities and nuances of expanding telecommunications services, particularly in regions where infrastructure is limited or non-existent.

As Onesimus deepened his involvement in telecommunications through 'Cyber Influx,' he identified a critical gap in the market: many communities in and around his area lacked access to stable and fast internet. This gap was not just a business opportunity; it represented a deeper societal issue of digital divide and inequality. Onesimus saw this as a chance to make a real difference, aligning with his ongoing commitment to use technology as a tool for empowerment.

This chapter details Onesimus's strategic approach to tackling this challenge. He began exploring various technologies that could facilitate internet connectivity in hard-to-reach areas. This exploration led him to consider options like satellite internet, long-range Wi-Fi, and other wireless communication technologies. Each option presented its own set of technical challenges, costs, and feasibility issues.

Onesimus's journey in addressing remote connectivity was filled with trials and experimentation. He had to navigate not only the technical aspects of setting up such networks but also deal with logistical and regulatory hurdles. Securing the necessary equipment, obtaining permits, and establishing partnerships with service providers were all part of the complex process.

The narrative also delves into the impact of Onesimus's efforts. Successfully establishing internet connectivity in remote areas was more than a business achievement; it was a step towards bridging the digital divide. His work enabled students in these areas to access educational resources, helped local businesses to tap into new markets, and allowed residents to connect with the wider world.

"The Challenge of Remote Connectivity" is a compelling story of resilience, innovation, and social responsibility. It showcases Onesimus's dedication to overcoming obstacles in pursuit of a larger goal – to bring technology and its benefits to underserved communities. This chapter not only highlights the technical and business aspects of expanding internet access but also underscores the transformative power of connectivity in enhancing lives and communities. For Onesimus, tackling the challenge of remote connectivity was a reaffirmation of his belief in technology as a force for good and an enabler of progress and equality.

SABOTAGE: BATTLING THE UNEXPECTED

"Sabotage: Battling the Unexpected" presents a dramatic turn in Onesimus Malatji's entrepreneurial journey, highlighting a challenging period where he faced unforeseen adversity. This chapter delves into the incidents of sabotage that Onesimus encountered in his telecommunications venture, showcasing his resilience and determination in the face of malicious actions that threatened his business.

As Onesimus worked tirelessly to establish remote connectivity solutions, his efforts were met with unexpected sabotage. Vital equipment, such as batteries and solar panels crucial for the wireless networks, were stolen or vandalized. These acts of sabotage were not just setbacks in terms of financial loss and delays, but they also posed a significant threat to the sustainability and credibility of his venture.

The narrative captures the initial shock and frustration that Onesimus experienced. Each incident of sabotage was a blow to his efforts to provide essential services to underserved communities. However, true to his character, Onesimus refused to be deterred. He recognized that these challenges were part of the risk of doing business, especially in an industry as critical and impactful as telecommunications.

Onesimus's response to the sabotage was multifaceted. He increased security measures, installing surveillance systems and enhancing physical protections for the equipment. He also reached out to the community, engaging with local leaders and residents to raise awareness about the importance of the infrastructure and how its damage was detrimental to everyone.

This chapter also explores the emotional and psychological toll of battling sabotage. Onesimus had to navigate not only the practical aspects of replacing and protecting his equipment but also the sense of betrayal and frustration that came with each act of vandalism. Despite these challenges, his commitment to his mission never wavered.

"Sabotage: Battling the Unexpected" is a poignant reminder of the hurdles entrepreneurs can face, often from unforeseen and external sources. It illustrates Onesimus's strength in adversity, his ability to adapt to challenging situations, and his unwavering focus on his goals. This chapter is not just about the physical acts of sabotage but also about overcoming obstacles, staying resilient in the face of adversity, and the importance of community support and engagement in ensuring the success of a business venture.

THE MTN SOUTH AFRICA PARTNERSHIP

"The MTN South Africa Partnership" recounts a significant strategic move in Onesimus Malatji's business journey, highlighting his collaboration with MTN South Africa, one of the leading telecommunications companies in the region. This chapter explores the intricacies of forging a partnership with a major industry player, underscoring Onesimus's strategic vision and his ability to navigate complex business landscapes.

Following the challenges of establishing remote connectivity and combating sabotage, Onesimus recognized the need for a robust partnership that could enhance the scale and impact of his telecommunications venture. The partnership with MTN South Africa represented a major leap, providing a platform for Onesimus to expand his services and leverage the expertise and infrastructure of a well-established telecom giant.

This chapter delves into the negotiation and establishment of the partnership. Onesimus approached MTN South Africa with a proposal that outlined the mutual benefits of collaboration. For MTN, partnering with Onesimus's enterprise offered an opportunity to expand their reach into markets and communities they were less familiar with. For Onesimus, this partnership meant access to cutting-edge technology, technical support, and a broader service portfolio.

The narrative highlights the challenges and learning experiences that came with managing such a partnership. Onesimus had to navigate corporate dynamics, align business objectives, and manage expectations on both sides. The process required him to blend his entrepreneurial agility with the more structured corporate strategies of MTN.

One of the key aspects of this partnership was the development of tailored solutions that leveraged MTN's technological capabilities to meet the specific needs of Onesimus's target communities. This collaboration led to the introduction of innovative services that significantly improved connectivity and digital access in underserved areas.

"The MTN South Africa Partnership" is a testament to Onesimus's growth as an entrepreneur. It showcases his strategic thinking, adaptability, and commitment to his vision of bridging the digital divide. This chapter not only highlights the potential of strategic partnerships in scaling business operations but also reflects Onesimus's dedication to leveraging such collaborations for the greater good of his community. The partnership with MTN South Africa was more than a business achievement; it was a step towards realizing a larger goal of inclusive technological advancement.

DREAMS UNRAVEL: THE PARTNERSHIP FAILS

"Dreams Unravel: The Partnership Fails" is a poignant chapter in Onesimus Malatji's entrepreneurial story, capturing a period of disappointment and reflection. Despite the initial promise and potential of the partnership with MTN South Africa, this chapter details how the collaboration ultimately fell short of expectations, leading to its eventual dissolution.

The unravelling of the partnership was a gradual process, marked by a series of challenges and misunderstandings. Initially, the collaboration between Onesimus's enterprise and MTN South Africa had been a source of optimism. It was seen as a strategic alliance that would bring advanced telecommunications solutions to underserved communities while expanding the reach of both parties. However, as the partnership progressed, issues began to surface.

One of the key challenges was the misalignment of priorities and expectations. Onesimus had entered the partnership with a vision of creating widespread impact and accessibility, while MTN South Africa, as a large corporation, had different operational and financial priorities. This divergence in objectives led to conflicts and frustration on both sides.

The narrative delves into the specific incidents and decisions that exacerbated the tensions. There were delays and bureaucratic hurdles that hindered project implementations, disagreements over resource allocation, and differences in approach to market engagement and community involvement. These issues, compounded over time, led to a growing sense of disillusionment for Onesimus.

Onesimus's personal and professional journey during this period was complex. He grappled with the realization that the partnership he had invested so much hope and effort in was not yielding the results he had envisioned. The chapter explores the emotional toll of this realization, the sense of responsibility he felt towards his community, and the difficult decision to step away from the partnership.

"Dreams Unravel: The Partnership Fails" is a chapter about resilience in the face of setbacks and the importance of staying true to one's vision, even when it means making tough decisions. It illustrates the challenges inherent in collaborations between small enterprises and large corporations, and the realities of navigating corporate partnerships. For Onesimus, the end of the partnership with MTN South Africa was not just the closure of a business chapter; it was a learning experience that reinforced the importance of aligning values and objectives in business collaborations. Despite the disappointment, this period was a catalyst for Onesimus to refocus on his goals and recommit to his mission of using technology to empower communities.

WRITING: A NEW CHAPTER

"Writing: A New Chapter" unfolds as a transformative period in Onesimus Malatji's journey, showcasing his shift from the tangible world of telecommunications and technology to the introspective and reflective realm of writing. This chapter captures Onesimus's transition into authorship, a pathway that allowed him to express his experiences, insights, and visions in a new, creative format.

After the dissolution of the partnership with MTN South Africa, Onesimus found himself at a crossroads. The experience, while challenging, sparked a period of deep introspection and reassessment of his career and personal goals. It was during this reflective phase that he discovered a new avenue for his creativity and entrepreneurial spirit: writing.

Onesimus embarked on his writing journey with a wealth of experiences to share. His foray into authorship was driven by a desire to document his entrepreneurial journey, the lessons he had learned, and his insights into the world of technology and business. He saw writing as a medium to reach a broader audience, sharing his story to inspire, educate, and guide others who might be embarking on similar paths.

This chapter details the process of Onesimus crafting his first manuscript. He tackled writing with the same determination and self-taught ethos that had driven his success in business. Writing became a therapeutic exercise for him, a way to process his experiences and distil his learning into words. He delved into topics ranging from the challenges of entrepreneurship, the impact of technology on society, to the importance of resilience and adaptability.

The narrative explores the challenges Onesimus faced in this new venture. Writing required a different set of skills than he was accustomed to, and he had to navigate the world of publishing, an industry vastly different from technology and telecommunications. Despite these challenges, his commitment to sharing his story propelled him forward.

"Writing: A New Chapter" is a testament to Onesimus's evolving identity as an entrepreneur and his unceasing pursuit of growth and self-expression. It showcases his journey as a continuous process of learning and reinvention. This chapter illustrates how writing not only provided Onesimus with a platform to reflect on his journey but also opened up new opportunities for him to impact and connect with a wider audience. Through his writing, Onesimus continued to contribute to the fields he was passionate about, while also exploring new dimensions of his creativity and entrepreneurial spirit.

THE JOURNEY TO 147 BOOKS

"The Journey to 147 Books" is an extraordinary chapter in Onesimus Malatji's story, chronicling his prolific journey as an author. From the inception of his writing career, Onesimus embarked on an ambitious path, resulting in the remarkable achievement of publishing 147 books. This chapter highlights his prolific output, the themes and subjects of his writings, and the impact of his work.

Onesimus's transition to writing was more than a change of pace; it became a conduit for his vast array of experiences and insights. Each book he wrote was a reflection of different facets of his life - his entrepreneurial ventures, the lessons learned from successes and failures, and his deep understanding of technology and its societal impacts. His writings covered a broad spectrum, from business and technology to motivational and personal development themes.

The process of writing 147 books was a testament to Onesimus's discipline, creativity, and dedication. This chapter delves into his writing process, revealing how he drew upon his experiences to create content that was both informative and inspiring. Onesimus approached writing with the same entrepreneurial spirit that he had applied to his businesses. He set ambitious goals, adhered to strict writing schedules, and continuously sought new ideas and perspectives to share with his readers.

Onesimus's books gained a wide readership, appealing to a diverse audience, including aspiring entrepreneurs, technology enthusiasts, and general readers seeking inspiration and guidance. His ability to distil complex ideas into accessible and engaging prose contributed significantly to his popularity as an author.

This chapter also explores the challenges Onesimus faced in the publishing world. Navigating the complexities of book production, distribution, and marketing required him to learn and adapt quickly. Despite these challenges, his commitment to sharing his knowledge and experiences remained unwavering.

"The Journey to 147 Books" is a celebration of Onesimus Malatji's enduring commitment to learning, sharing knowledge, and inspiring others. His journey as an author is not just about the impressive number of books published; it is about the impact and legacy of his writings. Through his books, Onesimus established himself as a thought leader and a source of inspiration for countless individuals. His journey underscores the power of storytelling and the written word in sharing knowledge, inspiring change, and leaving a lasting impact.

EMBRACING THE DIGITAL AGE

"Embracing the Digital Age" is a pivotal chapter in Onesimus Malatji's story, highlighting his adaptation and integration into the rapidly evolving digital world. This chapter encapsulates how Onesimus, leveraging his vast experience in technology and telecommunications, embraced new digital trends and technologies to further his entrepreneurial ventures and authorial pursuits.

The digital age, characterized by rapid technological advancements and a shift towards an increasingly connected world, presented both challenges and opportunities for Onesimus. Recognizing the potential of digital platforms, he began exploring ways to integrate these tools into his business strategies and writing endeavours.

In his businesses, particularly in 'Cyber Influx,' Onesimus embraced digital technologies to enhance operational efficiency and customer engagement. He implemented digital systems for better service delivery, used social media for marketing and community engagement, and explored e-commerce platforms to expand his customer base. This digital integration allowed him to reach a wider audience and offer more comprehensive services.

As an author, Onesimus recognized the significance of the digital landscape in publishing. He delved into the world of e-books and digital content, understanding that these platforms offered a way to reach a global audience. Onesimus adapted his writing and publishing strategies to align with digital trends, making his books available in various digital formats and harnessing online marketing tools to promote his work.

This chapter also explores how Onesimus used digital platforms to share knowledge and inspire others. He started a blog and engaged in online forums, offering advice and insights on entrepreneurship, technology, and personal development. Through these platforms, he connected with a broader audience, offering mentorship and guidance.

"Embracing the Digital Age" reflects Onesimus's agility and foresight in navigating the digital landscape. It showcases his ability to continuously evolve and adapt his strategies to stay relevant and competitive. This chapter is a testament to the importance of embracing change and innovation in the digital era. For Onesimus, the digital age was not just a new set of tools and platforms; it represented a new realm of possibilities to grow his businesses, share his story, and make a more significant impact.

LIFE'S UNPREDICTABLE NATURE

"Life's Unpredictable Nature" is a reflective chapter in Onesimus Malatji's journey, underscoring the often-unforeseen twists and turns that life can present. This chapter delves into the personal and professional challenges Onesimus faced, highlighting his resilience and adaptability in the face of uncertainty and change.

Throughout his entrepreneurial and authorial pursuits, Onesimus encountered numerous unexpected events that tested his resolve and forced him to revaluate his path. These included not only business-related challenges like market fluctuations and technological disruptions but also personal trials that impacted his professional life.

One of the key themes of this chapter is how Onesimus navigated these unpredictable waters. He faced each challenge with a blend of pragmatism and optimism, using his experiences as learning opportunities. This mindset helped him to not only overcome difficulties but also to grow stronger and wiser from them.

This chapter also explores the emotional aspects of dealing with uncertainty. Onesimus's journey was not just about business strategies and innovation; it was also about personal growth and developing emotional resilience. He learned to embrace the unpredictable nature of life, understanding that it often brings both challenges and opportunities.

"Life's Unpredictable Nature" is a testament to the fact that adaptability and resilience are crucial for long-term success and fulfilment. It showcases Onesimus's journey as a continuous process of learning, adaptation, and growth. Through his story, he inspires others to embrace life's unpredictability, to find strength in adversity, and to remain open to new possibilities and paths. This chapter not only highlights Onesimus's entrepreneurial spirit but also his ability to navigate the complex and often uncertain journey of life with grace and determination.

THE BURDEN OF LOSS

"The Burden of Loss" is a deeply introspective and poignant chapter in Onesimus Malatji's journey, where he confronts and grapples with various forms of loss. This chapter sheds light on the emotional and psychological impact of experiencing setbacks, both in his personal life and professional ventures, revealing a more vulnerable and resilient aspect of his character.

In this phase of his life, Onesimus faced significant losses that tested his strength and resilience. Professionally, the dissolution of key partnerships, the challenges in his telecommunications venture, and the fluctuating fortunes of his businesses posed not just financial strains but also took an emotional toll. Each setback in his professional journey was a lesson in endurance and perseverance, but it also brought a sense of loss and disappointment.

Personal losses also cast a shadow during this period. Onesimus encountered life events that brought grief and sorrow, profoundly affecting his outlook and approach to life and business. The chapter explores how these personal experiences of loss influenced his professional decisions and his interactions with those around him.

Despite these challenges, "The Burden of Loss" is also about resilience and recovery. Onesimus's journey through periods of loss is marked by introspection, learning, and a gradual rebuilding of his life and ventures. He learns to cope with the emotional aspects of loss, finding ways to channel his experiences into renewed motivation and perspective.

This chapter also touches upon the universal nature of loss and the importance of support systems during tough times. Onesimus's story becomes a source of inspiration, showcasing his ability to navigate through life's trials with grace and fortitude. It highlights how personal and professional setbacks, while challenging, can also lead to growth, new insights, and renewed determination.

"The Burden of Loss" is a poignant reminder of the complexities of the entrepreneurial journey and the human experience. It demonstrates that facing and overcoming adversity is an integral part of life's journey, shaping one's character and path in profound ways. For Onesimus, these experiences of loss and the lessons learned from them contributed significantly to his maturity as an individual and as an entrepreneur, reinforcing his resilience and capacity for adaptation.

RELEARNING THE BUSINESS WORLD

"Relearning the Business World" is a pivotal chapter in Onesimus Malatji's story, highlighting a phase of recalibration and renewed learning in his entrepreneurial journey. Following the setbacks and personal challenges detailed in "The Burden of Loss," Onesimus finds himself in a period of introspection, leading to a re-examination and evolution of his approach to business.

In this chapter, Onesimus embarks on a journey to reacquaint himself with the ever-changing landscape of the business world. The rapid advancements in technology, shifts in market dynamics, and his own personal experiences necessitated a fresh perspective on how to navigate the complexities of entrepreneurship.

This narrative explores Onesimus's proactive steps to update his knowledge and skills. He delves into new studies and research, attends workshops and seminars, and engages with other entrepreneurs to exchange ideas and experiences. This process of continuous learning is not just about acquiring new information; it's about adapting to new methodologies, technologies, and business models.

The chapter also reflects on how Onesimus applied these learnings to revitalize his existing ventures and explore new opportunities. He revisited his business strategies, incorporating more digital tools and platforms to enhance efficiency and reach.

He also explored new markets and niches, applying his accrued wisdom to innovate and diversify his business portfolio. "Relearning the Business World" is a testament to Onesimus's resilience and his commitment to growth and adaptation.

It showcases his recognition that learning is a lifelong process, especially in the ever-evolving world of business. This period of re-education and realignment was crucial in preparing Onesimus for the next phase of his entrepreneurial journey, equipping him with the tools, knowledge, and mindset needed to tackle new challenges and seize new opportunities.

This chapter is not just about business acumen; it's about the importance of staying agile and open-minded in a world of constant change. It illustrates how personal setbacks can be transformed into opportunities for growth and how continuous learning is key to long-term success and fulfilment in the business world. For Onesimus, relearning the business world was an essential step in his journey, enabling him to emerge stronger, wiser, and more prepared for the future.

NAVIGATING THROUGH INDUSTRY MANIPULATION

"Navigating Through Industry Manipulation" is a critical chapter in Onesimus Malatji's entrepreneurial journey, spotlighting the challenges he faced in an environment rife with competition and underhanded tactics. This chapter delves into Onesimus's experiences with manipulation in the business world, showcasing his strategic thinking and ethical stance in navigating these tricky waters.

Onesimus encountered various forms of manipulation as he expanded his business ventures, particularly in the telecommunications and tech sectors. These manipulations ranged from unfair competitive practices and market monopolization to more direct attempts by larger entities to undercut or sabotage his business. These experiences were a harsh introduction to some of the more unethical aspects of the industry.

In this chapter, Onesimus shares how he identified and responded to such manipulative tactics. He relied heavily on his acute business acumen, gathering information and analysing market trends to understand the underlying motivations and strategies of his competitors. This intelligence allowed him to anticipate potential manipulations and prepare accordingly.

One of the key themes of this chapter is the importance of maintaining integrity in business. Onesimus faced difficult decisions, often having to choose between potentially lucrative opportunities and his ethical principles. He chose to uphold his values, believing that long-term success was rooted in fair and transparent business practices.

Onesimus's approach to dealing with industry manipulation involved strengthening his business from within. He focused on building a loyal customer base through excellent service and trustworthy practices, diversified his business to reduce vulnerability, and formed strategic alliances with like-minded partners.

"Navigating Through Industry Manipulation" is a testament to Onesimus's resilience and ethical fortitude in the face of challenging industry dynamics. It highlights the complexities of operating in competitive business environments and the necessity of strategic planning, vigilance, and ethical decision-making. This chapter is not just about the challenges of manipulation but also about the strength and integrity required to navigate them successfully. For Onesimus, these experiences underscored the importance of staying true to his principles while adeptly navigating the often-murky waters of the business world.

THE PERILS OF ENVY AND BETRAYAL

"The Perils of Envy and Betrayal" is a profound chapter in Onesimus Malatji's narrative, exploring the darker aspects of human nature he encountered in his business journey. This chapter delves into the personal and professional impact of envy and betrayal, experiences that tested his resilience and integrity in the highly competitive business world.

As Onesimus's ventures grew in success and visibility, they inadvertently attracted not only admiration and respect but also envy and jealousy from some quarters. This envy sometimes manifested in harmful ways, including attempts by competitors and even acquaintances to undermine his achievements or to take advantage of his trust.

The chapter provides insights into specific instances where Onesimus faced betrayal. These betrayals ranged from intellectual property theft and underhanded competitive tactics to breaches of trust within his inner professional circle. Each instance was a blow to Onesimus, challenging his faith in people and shaking the foundations of his professional relationships.

Onesimus's response to these challenges was a blend of strategic action and personal reflection. Professionally, he reinforced his business practices, tightening security measures and becoming more circumspect in his partnerships and collaborations. He also sought legal recourse where necessary to protect his business interests.

On a personal level, Onesimus grappled with the emotional repercussions of these experiences. He learned hard lessons about human nature, trust, and the importance of vigilance in business dealings. Despite these setbacks, he refused to let cynicism cloud his judgment or to compromise his principles of fairness and integrity.

"The Perils of Envy and Betrayal" is a raw and honest account of the challenges entrepreneurs can face from external envy and internal betrayal. It underscores the importance of resilience, cautious trust, and the strength of character in the face of such challenges. This chapter adds depth to Onesimus's story, highlighting not only his business acumen but also his capacity to navigate complex human dynamics. It's a testament to his ability to overcome personal and professional trials and to emerge stronger and more insightful.

THE POWER OF CREATING AND INNOVATING

"The Power of Creating and Innovating" is a chapter that celebrates Onesimus Malatji's relentless spirit of innovation and creativity, pivotal elements that have consistently fuelled his entrepreneurial journey. This part of his narrative underscores his ability to continuously generate new ideas, adapt to changing environments, and create solutions that address evolving market needs.

In the face of the adversities described in previous chapters, including industry manipulation and personal betrayals, Onesimus's response was not to retreat but to innovate. He saw challenges as opportunities to think creatively and to develop innovative solutions that set his ventures apart from the competition.

This chapter details the various ways in which Onesimus harnessed his creative and innovative abilities. In his telecommunications venture, for example, he constantly explored emerging technologies and found inventive ways to integrate them into his services, enhancing customer experience and expanding his market reach.

In the realm of writing and publishing, Onesimus's innovation was reflected in how he approached content creation and distribution. He experimented with different genres and formats, reaching wider audiences through digital platforms, and engaging readers with interactive and dynamic content.

One of the key themes of this chapter is Onesimus's belief in the transformative power of innovation. He understood that in the fast-paced world of technology and business, stagnation meant falling behind. His commitment to innovation was not just about staying competitive; it was about leading change and shaping the future of his industry.

"The Power of Creating and Innovating" also delves into the personal satisfaction Onesimus derived from the creative process. For him, innovation was not merely a business strategy; it was a form of self-expression and fulfilment. It was his way of leaving a mark on the world, of making a difference through his ideas and creations.

This chapter is a testament to Onesimus's visionary approach and his unyielding drive to create and innovate. It highlights how creativity and innovation are vital for business growth and sustainability. For Onesimus, these traits were key to navigating the complexities of the business world and to building a legacy that transcends the norm. His story in this chapter serves as an inspiration for aspiring entrepreneurs and innovators, illustrating that the power to create and innovate can lead to remarkable achievements and enduring impact.

RISING LIKE A PHOENIX

"Rising Like a Phoenix" is a metaphorically rich chapter in Onesimus Malatji's life story, symbolizing his remarkable ability to emerge stronger and more determined from setbacks and failures. This chapter encapsulates the resilience and tenacity with which Onesimus approached each challenge, reaffirming his unwavering spirit in the face of adversity.

Throughout his journey, Onesimus encountered numerous obstacles – from the early challenges in his telecommunications endeavours to the complexities and betrayals in the business world. Each of these instances, while daunting, served as a catalyst for Onesimus to reassess, reinvent, and rejuvenate his strategies and ambitions.

This chapter details how Onesimus, much like a phoenix rising from the ashes, used his setbacks as opportunities for growth and learning. After the dissolution of partnerships and the personal losses he experienced, he did not succumb to despair. Instead, he drew strength from these experiences, using them to fuel his passion for innovation and his commitment to his ventures.

"Rising Like a Phoenix" also explores the transformative processes Onesimus underwent. He continually adapted his business models, embracing new technologies and market trends, and diversified his interests to mitigate risks and tap into new opportunities.

This adaptability was not just a business strategy; it was a reflection of his personal growth and evolving mindset. Furthermore, the chapter touches on the inspirational aspect of Onesimus's journey. His resilience in overcoming hardships and rebuilding from losses has made him a figure of inspiration and a role model for other entrepreneurs and individuals facing their own trials. Onesimus's story of rising again after each fall resonates with the universal human experience of facing and overcoming adversity.

The narrative of "Rising Like a Phoenix" is a powerful reminder of the strength of the human spirit and the endless potential for renewal and reinvention. It highlights Onesimus Malatji's journey not just as a tale of business success, but as a testament to the enduring power of resilience, adaptability, and perseverance. His ability to rise from the ashes of his challenges embodies the essence of true entrepreneurial spirit and serves as a beacon of hope and inspiration for many.

OVERCOMING LIFE'S DEMONS

"Overcoming Life's Demons" is a deeply introspective chapter in Onesimus Malatji's narrative, where he confronts and tackles the internal struggles and personal challenges that have accompanied his entrepreneurial journey. This chapter goes beyond the external business battles to reveal Onesimus's resilience in dealing with his inner demons – be they doubt, fear, or the aftermath of personal and professional setbacks.

Throughout his career, Onesimus faced not just business-related adversities but also personal trials that tested his mental and emotional fortitude. This chapter delves into how he coped with the pressures of entrepreneurship, the stress of constant innovation, and the emotional toll of navigating a complex and often ruthless business landscape.

One of the core aspects of this chapter is Onesimus's candid reflection on the moments of self-doubt and uncertainty. Despite his successes, he grappled with the 'impostor syndrome' and the fear of failure. He opens up about the times he questioned his decisions and the impact of these doubts on his mental health and personal life.

Onesimus's journey through these internal battles is marked by a growing awareness and understanding of the importance of mental and emotional well-being.

He shares the strategies and coping mechanisms he developed – from seeking mentorship and advice to embracing mindfulness and self-care practices. He highlights the role of a supportive network, including family, friends, and professional counsellors, in helping him navigate through darker times.

"Overcoming Life's Demons" also addresses the universal nature of these challenges. Onesimus's experiences resonate with many entrepreneurs and individuals who face similar internal struggles. His openness in discussing these issues serves to destigmatize mental health challenges, particularly in the entrepreneurial community, where they are often overlooked or hidden.

This chapter is a powerful narrative of personal growth and inner strength. It showcases Onesimus's journey not just as a series of business achievements but as a continuous process of personal development and overcoming. It underscores the message that facing and conquering one's inner demons is as crucial as overcoming external challenges. For Onesimus, this journey of overcoming has been essential in shaping him into a more resilient, empathetic, and grounded individual and leader.

THE STRUGGLE WITH LICENSING AND REGULATIONS

"The Struggle with Licensing and Regulations" presents a crucial aspect of Onesimus Malatji's entrepreneurial journey, highlighting the challenges he faced in navigating the complex and often cumbersome world of business licensing and regulatory compliance. This chapter illustrates the hurdles that Onesimus encountered in ensuring that his ventures adhered to the necessary legal and bureaucratic standards, a common yet daunting task for many entrepreneurs.

Onesimus's foray into various sectors, especially telecommunications, required him to deal with a myriad of regulations and licensing requirements. These ranged from obtaining permissions to operate certain technologies to adhering to industry-specific legal standards. The process was often laden with red tape, requiring a significant investment of time, resources, and patience.

This chapter details the specific challenges Onesimus faced in acquiring and maintaining the necessary licenses for his businesses. These included navigating unclear regulatory frameworks, dealing with lengthy approval processes, and sometimes encountering seemingly arbitrary bureaucratic hurdles. The costs associated with these processes also posed a significant burden, especially for a growing enterprise.

One of the key themes of this chapter is Onesimus's perseverance and resourcefulness in tackling these challenges. He took proactive steps to understand the legal requirements, sought advice from experts, and even engaged with regulatory bodies to advocate for more streamlined processes. His approach was a blend of compliance and advocacy – ensuring his businesses met legal standards while also pushing for a more conducive regulatory environment for entrepreneurs.

"The Struggle with Licensing and Regulations" also touches on the broader implications of these challenges for the business community. Onesimus's experiences reflect a common struggle among entrepreneurs and highlight the need for more supportive and transparent regulatory frameworks to foster business growth and innovation.

This chapter is a testament to the often-overlooked but critical aspect of entrepreneurship: navigating the legal and regulatory landscapes. It underscores the importance of diligence, legal awareness, and adaptability in the face of bureaucratic challenges. For Onesimus, the struggle with licensing and regulations was not just a hurdle to overcome but also an opportunity to learn, grow, and contribute to the betterment of the business environment for his and other enterprises.

THE WEIGHT OF FINANCIAL BURDENS

"The Weight of Financial Burdens" is a chapter that delves into one of the most challenging aspects of Onesimus Malatji's entrepreneurial journey: managing the financial pressures that come with running a business. This part of his story is a candid exploration of the fiscal challenges he faced, from cash flow management to funding growth, and how these pressures tested his resilience and business acumen.

Throughout his various ventures, Onesimus encountered numerous financial hurdles. These ranged from initial funding issues in starting and expanding his businesses, to managing the operational costs of running technologically advanced enterprises like his telecommunications venture and Cyber Influx.

This chapter provides an in-depth look at the financial realities of entrepreneurship. Onesimus grappled with maintaining a healthy cash flow, balancing the need to reinvest in the business with the necessity of covering day-to-day expenses. He faced high upfront costs for technology and equipment, not to mention the ongoing expenses of upgrades and maintenance. Additionally, Onesimus had to navigate the challenges of securing loans or investment, often in a financial market sceptical of small business risks.

One of the key themes of "The Weight of Financial Burdens" is the constant juggling act Onesimus performed to keep his businesses financially viable. This often meant making tough decisions – cutting costs, delaying expansion plans, or even pivoting business strategies to align with financial realities.

Onesimus's approach to these financial challenges was marked by creativity and pragmatism. He explored various funding avenues, from traditional bank loans to more innovative financing methods like partnerships and venture capital. He also developed strict financial management practices, keeping close track of expenses and revenue streams.

This chapter also touches on the emotional and psychological impact of financial stress. Onesimus candidly shares the pressure and anxiety associated with financial uncertainties, and how this aspect of business ownership can be as challenging as any operational or market issue.

"The Weight of Financial Burdens" is a relatable and insightful look into the financial trials of entrepreneurship. It underscores the importance of financial literacy, careful planning, and adaptability in managing a business's fiscal health. For Onesimus, overcoming these financial challenges was a crucial part of his growth as an entrepreneur, providing valuable lessons in resilience and fiscal responsibility.

REDISCOVERING PURPOSE

"Rediscovering Purpose" is a reflective and transformative chapter in Onesimus Malatji's narrative, marking a period of introspection and realignment with his core values and motivations. After navigating a series of professional challenges and personal trials, Onesimus finds himself revisiting the fundamental reasons behind his entrepreneurial journey, seeking to reconnect with the passions that originally fuelled his ambitions.

This chapter unfolds as Onesimus takes a step back from the immediate pressures and demands of business management to ponder deeper questions about his life's work. He reflects on what success truly means to him, beyond financial gains and business growth. This introspective journey leads him to reassess not just his business goals, but also his broader impact on society and his legacy.

One of the key themes of "Rediscovering Purpose" is the realization that true fulfilment in entrepreneurship goes beyond monetary achievements. Onesimus revisits the initial spark that led him to start his ventures – the desire to make a difference, to innovate, and to contribute positively to his community. He contemplates how his businesses can be vehicles for social change, technological advancement, and empowerment.

The narrative also captures Onesimus's efforts to realign his business practices with his rediscovered purpose. He begins to prioritize projects and initiatives that have a meaningful impact, focusing on ventures that align with his values and aspirations. This might involve supporting local communities, investing in sustainable practices, or mentoring young entrepreneurs.

This chapter is also about balance – balancing the pursuit of profit with the pursuit of purpose. Onesimus strives to find harmony between running successful businesses and staying true to his vision of making a positive mark in the world. He recognizes that his entrepreneurial journey is not just a business endeavour, but a personal journey of growth, learning, and fulfilment.

"Rediscovering Purpose" is a poignant reminder of the importance of staying connected to one's core motivations. It highlights Onesimus's resilience, not just in facing external business challenges, but in confronting and overcoming internal conflicts and dilemmas. This chapter serves as an inspiration for entrepreneurs and individuals alike, underscoring the power of purpose in driving meaningful and fulfilling endeavours. For Onesimus, this period of rediscovery was not just a momentary pause; it was a crucial pivot that redefined his path and reignited his passion for his work.

THE DRIVE FOR FULFILMENT

"The Drive for Fulfilment" is a deeply personal chapter in Onesimus Malatji's story, where he focuses on achieving a sense of fulfilment that transcends the typical metrics of business success. After encountering various professional and personal challenges, Onesimus embarks on a journey to understand and achieve true fulfilment in his life and career.

This chapter explores Onesimus's realization that while financial success and business growth are important, they do not necessarily equate to personal fulfilment. He reflects on the journey he has undertaken, the highs and lows, and starts to question what brings him genuine satisfaction and joy.

A key element of this chapter is Onesimus's exploration of what fulfilment means to him. He considers the impact of his work on others, the legacy he wishes to leave behind, and how his business endeavours align with his personal values and life goals. This introspection leads him to redefine his measures of success, focusing more on the positive impact he can have on individuals and communities.

Onesimus begins to shift his approach to business, prioritizing projects and initiatives that have a meaningful and lasting impact. This could involve mentoring emerging entrepreneurs, engaging in community projects, or focusing on sustainable and socially responsible business practices.

The narrative also details how Onesimus seeks fulfilment outside the realm of business. He explores personal interests and passions that had been side-lined in his pursuit of business success. This could involve artistic pursuits, spending more time with family and friends, or engaging in philanthropic activities.

"The Drive for Fulfilment" is about Onesimus's realization that fulfilment is a multifaceted and deeply personal journey. It illustrates the importance of aligning one's professional endeavours with personal values and finding joy in the journey itself, not just the destination. This chapter is a testament to the fact that true fulfilment often lies in the balance between personal and professional life, and in making a positive difference in the lives of others.

For Onesimus, this drive for fulfilment redefines his approach to life and business, leading to a more holistic and satisfying journey. It's a powerful message about the importance of seeking fulfilment in all aspects of life, and a reminder that success can be measured in many ways, not just in financial terms.

THE VOID OF LOSS

"The Void of Loss" is a poignant and introspective chapter in Onesimus Malatji's narrative, focusing on the profound sense of emptiness and grief that follows significant personal and professional losses. This chapter explores the emotional landscape of Onesimus as he confronts the void left by these losses, delving into the complex process of mourning and finding meaning in the aftermath.

Onesimus's journey has been marked not only by entrepreneurial triumphs but also by moments of profound loss. These losses ranged from the failure of business ventures and the dissolution of partnerships to deeply personal losses, such as the death of close associates, friends, or family members. Each loss carved a deep emotional void, challenging his resilience and forcing him to confront feelings of sorrow, grief, and sometimes, isolation.

This chapter thoughtfully explores the impact of these losses on Onesimus's personal and professional life. It reveals how grief can affect one's worldview, decision-making process, and overall sense of purpose. Onesimus finds himself grappling with questions about the impermanence of success and the fragility of human connections.

In "The Void of Loss," Onesimus also embarks on a journey of healing and self-discovery. He engages in introspection, seeking to understand and process his grief.

This period involves a re-evaluation of his priorities and a renewed appreciation for the transient nature of life and business. Onesimus learns to find solace in the memories of good times and the lessons learned from the challenges faced.

One significant aspect of this chapter is how Onesimus uses his experiences with loss to empathize with others going through similar situations. His own journey through the void of loss deepens his compassion and understanding, driving him to support others in their times of grief and difficulty.

"The Void of Loss" is a raw and honest depiction of the emotional toll of loss. It underscores the importance of acknowledging and dealing with grief, and the role of such experiences in shaping one's character and outlook on life. For Onesimus, navigating through the void of loss is a transformative process, leading to greater emotional depth, resilience, and a more profound understanding of the human experience.

CONFRONTING DEATH AND LEGACY

"Confronting Death and Legacy" is a deeply contemplative chapter in Onesimus Malatji's life story, where he grapples with the reality of mortality and its implications for his personal and professional legacy. This chapter explores Onesimus's reflections on the inevitability of death and how it shapes his perspective on life, his business decisions, and the legacy he wishes to leave behind.

Onesimus confronts the concept of death not as a distant abstraction but as a tangible presence that has touched his life and the lives of those around him. This confrontation is triggered by personal losses or moments when he comes face-to-face with his own mortality. These experiences provoke a profound revaluation of his life's priorities and the impact he wants to have on the world.

One of the key themes of this chapter is the idea of legacy. Onesimus contemplates what it means to leave a lasting impact. He reflects on how his entrepreneurial ventures, writings, and personal interactions will endure beyond his lifetime. This reflection leads him to consider the values he wants to embody and the memories he wishes to leave in the minds of those who know him.

In his businesses, Onesimus begins to place greater emphasis on projects and initiatives that have long-term value and contribute positively to society. He thinks about the kind of mentorship and knowledge he imparts to younger entrepreneurs, seeing these actions as part of the legacy he leaves in the business world.

On a personal level, Onesimus's confrontation with death inspires him to strengthen relationships with family and friends, to express gratitude and appreciation, and to live a life that is true to his beliefs and values. He becomes more mindful of the present, cherishing each moment and the opportunities to make a meaningful difference.

"Confronting Death and Legacy" is a chapter that highlights the human side of entrepreneurship – the fears, hopes, and reflections that lie beyond business success. It illustrates how the awareness of mortality can be a powerful motivator for living a life of purpose and intention. For Onesimus, confronting death becomes a catalyst for examining and solidifying his legacy, ensuring that his life's work resonates and endures beyond his time. This chapter is a poignant reminder of the importance of considering one's legacy in both personal and professional realms, inspiring a life lived with purpose and meaning.

BUILDING A LIFE BEYOND MATERIAL SUCCESS

"Building a Life Beyond Material Success" is a reflective and forward-looking chapter in Onesimus Malatji's story, where he shifts focus from the pursuit of material and business achievements to cultivating a life rich in experiences, relationships, and personal growth. This chapter explores Onesimus's journey towards finding balance and fulfilment beyond the traditional markers of success.

Throughout his entrepreneurial career, Onesimus achieved notable business milestones and accumulated material successes. However, this chapter marks a point where he begins to question the depth and value of these achievements. He ponders the broader aspects of life that contribute to genuine contentment and fulfilment.

One significant aspect of this chapter is Onesimus's exploration of non-material pursuits that enrich his life. He engages more deeply in hobbies and interests that had taken a back seat during his relentless pursuit of business success. This could include artistic endeavours, exploring nature, or dedicating time to hobbies that bring him joy and relaxation.

Onesimus also recognizes the importance of nurturing relationships with family, friends, and his community. He invests time and energy in strengthening these bonds, understanding that relationships are fundamental to a well-rounded and fulfilling life.

He becomes more involved in community activities, offering mentorship, support, and leveraging his resources for community benefit.

This chapter also delves into the concept of self-actualization. Onesimus embarks on a journey of personal development, seeking to understand himself better and to align his actions with his core values and beliefs. He explores spiritual and philosophical concepts, seeking deeper meaning and purpose in his life.

"Building a Life Beyond Material Success" is a testament to Onesimus's maturing perspective on what it means to live a successful life. It underscores the realization that true success encompasses personal well-being, happiness, and making a positive impact on others. For Onesimus, this period is about redefining success, focusing on holistic growth, and building a life that is not just financially rewarding but also emotionally and spiritually fulfilling. This chapter inspires readers to consider their definitions of success and to recognize the multifaceted nature of a truly successful and rewarding life.

REDEFINING SUCCESS IN BUSINESS

"Redefining Success in Business" is a significant chapter in Onesimus Malatji's narrative, marking a shift in his approach to defining what success means in the context of entrepreneurship. This chapter illuminates Onesimus's evolving understanding of success, moving away from traditional metrics like profit and growth, and embracing a more holistic perspective that includes social impact, personal fulfilment, and ethical practices.

Throughout his entrepreneurial journey, Onesimus achieved considerable business milestones, but this chapter reflects a deeper introspection on what these achievements truly mean. He begins to question the conventional wisdom that equates success strictly with financial gain and market dominance.

One key element of this chapter is Onesimus's focus on the impact of his businesses on society and the environment. He starts to measure success not just by the bottom line but by the positive changes his ventures bring about. This includes creating job opportunities, fostering innovation, and contributing to the community's well-being.

Onesimus also re-evaluates the role of his businesses in promoting ethical practices and sustainability. He recognizes that true success involves operating in a manner that is not only profitable but also responsible and conscientious.

This shift leads him to integrate sustainable practices into his business operations and to prioritize transparency and ethics in his dealings. Another important aspect of this chapter is the balance between professional achievements and personal well-being.

Onesimus realizes that personal fulfilment and a sense of purpose are integral components of success. He begins to align his business endeavours with his personal values, ensuring that his work is not only financially rewarding but also personally enriching.

"Redefining Success in Business" is a reflection of Onesimus's maturity as an entrepreneur and a human being. It showcases his journey from pursuing traditional business success to adopting a more comprehensive view that encompasses a broader spectrum of values and impacts. This chapter encourages readers to think about the broader implications of their business activities and to redefine success in a way that aligns with their personal values and aspirations. For Onesimus, redefining success means building businesses that are not only profitable but also contribute positively to society and align with his deeper life goals.

THE ENTREPRENEUR'S RESILIENCE

"The Entrepreneur's Resilience" is a chapter that celebrates and examines the enduring resilience of Onesimus Malatji throughout his entrepreneurial journey. This part of his story is a testament to his ability to withstand various challenges and setbacks, maintaining his perseverance and determination in the face of adversity. It is a narrative that delves into the core qualities that define and drive a resilient entrepreneur.

This chapter explores the numerous obstacles Onesimus encountered over his career, ranging from financial struggles and market fluctuations to personal trials and professional betrayals. Each of these challenges tested his resilience, pushing him to his limits but also providing opportunities for growth and learning.

Central to this chapter is the concept of resilience as a crucial trait for any entrepreneur. Onesimus's journey demonstrates how resilience is not just about enduring hardships but also about adapting to change, learning from failures, and emerging stronger from each experience. He shows that resilience in entrepreneurship involves a combination of mental toughness, emotional stability, and the ability to remain focused on long-term goals despite short-term difficulties.

Onesimus's strategies for building and maintaining resilience are also highlighted in this chapter. These include maintaining a positive outlook, setting realistic yet ambitious goals, and cultivating a supportive network of mentors, peers, and family. Additionally, Onesimus emphasizes the importance of self-care and maintaining a healthy work-life balance, recognizing that personal well-being is integral to sustaining resilience.

"The Entrepreneur's Resilience" also touches upon the broader implications of resilience in the business world. Onesimus's experiences serve as an inspiration and guide for other entrepreneurs facing their own set of challenges. His story is a reminder that while the path of entrepreneurship is often fraught with difficulties, resilience can be a powerful tool in overcoming obstacles and achieving success.

This chapter is not just about surviving tough times; it's about thriving amidst challenges and using adversity as a catalyst for personal and professional growth. Onesimus's resilience is a key factor in his longevity and success as an entrepreneur, and it offers valuable lessons on the importance of perseverance, adaptability, and strength in the entrepreneurial journey.

A NEW VISION FOR THE FUTURE

"A New Vision for the Future" is a forward-looking chapter in Onesimus Malatji's story, where he charts a course for the next phase of his entrepreneurial journey. After navigating through a series of challenges and recalibrating his understanding of success and fulfilment, Onesimus sets his sights on new goals and aspirations, driven by a refined vision and a deeper understanding of his purpose.

This chapter captures Onesimus's reflective process as he envisions the future of his enterprises and his personal life. It's a period marked by strategic planning, creative thinking, and a rekindling of his passion for innovation and social impact.

One of the key elements of this new vision is a renewed commitment to leveraging technology for societal good. Onesimus recognizes the transformative power of technology and aims to harness it not just for business growth but also for addressing societal challenges. This may involve developing tech solutions for education, healthcare, or environmental sustainability, reflecting a broader and more impactful entrepreneurial ambition.

Onesimus also envisions expanding his mentorship and community involvement. Drawing on his wealth of experience, he sees himself playing a more significant role in nurturing the next generation of entrepreneurs.

This involves not only imparting business knowledge but also instilling values of resilience, ethical entrepreneurship, and the importance of balancing profit with purpose.

Another aspect of his future vision is a focus on global connectivity and collaboration. Onesimus plans to extend his reach beyond his local community, engaging with international partners and markets. This global perspective is driven by a desire to learn from diverse business cultures and to bring global insights back to his ventures.

"A New Vision for the Future" is also about personal growth and well-being. Onesimus places greater emphasis on his own health, relationships, and personal interests, recognizing that a fulfilled life is foundational to sustained success. He seeks to strike a balance that allows him to thrive both professionally and personally.

This chapter is a mosaic of ambition, wisdom, and aspiration. It shows Onesimus looking ahead with optimism and clarity, ready to embark on new adventures and challenges. His new vision for the future is not just a roadmap for his business endeavours but also a blueprint for a life of impact, growth, and fulfilment. It is a vision that encapsulates the lessons of the past and the hopes for the future, marking a new chapter in Onesimus's remarkable journey.

THE ESSENCE OF INNOVATION

"The Essence of Innovation" is a pivotal chapter in Onesimus Malatji's story, encapsulating his deep-seated belief in and commitment to innovation as a driving force in both his entrepreneurial ventures and personal growth. This chapter explores Onesimus's understanding of innovation not just as a business tool, but as a mindset and a way of life that continually pushes boundaries and challenges the status quo.

Throughout his diverse business endeavours, Onesimus has consistently demonstrated a knack for innovative thinking. This chapter delves into his philosophy that innovation is key to staying relevant and competitive in the rapidly changing business landscape. He sees innovation as the catalyst for growth, adaptation, and survival in the face of evolving market demands and technological advancements.

One of the core themes of this chapter is how Onesimus fosters a culture of innovation within his businesses. He encourages creative thinking, experimentation, and risk-taking, understanding that groundbreaking ideas often come from pushing beyond comfort zones. Onesimus also invests in research and development, staying abreast of emerging trends and technologies that can be harnessed to create new products, services, or business models.

Innovation for Onesimus also extends to his approach to problem-solving. He tackles challenges with a unique perspective, often finding unconventional solutions that are more effective and efficient. This creative problem-solving has been a key factor in overcoming many of the obstacles he has faced in his entrepreneurial journey.

"The Essence of Innovation" also highlights Onesimus's belief in the power of innovation to drive social change. He envisions using innovative solutions to address societal issues, from improving access to education and healthcare to promoting sustainable practices. Onesimus sees his role as an entrepreneur as not just to create profitable businesses but to make a positive impact on the world.

This chapter is a celebration of Onesimus's unyielding spirit of innovation. It underscores his conviction that continuous innovation is essential for personal and professional development. For Onesimus, innovation is more than a business strategy; it is a way of thinking and living that perpetually seeks to improve, disrupt, and advance. His commitment to innovation is a testament to his visionary approach and his unwavering pursuit of excellence and impact.

LEARNING FROM PAST MISTAKES

"Learning from Past Mistakes" is a reflective and insightful chapter in Onesimus Malatji's journey, emphasizing the crucial role that past errors and misjudgements have played in shaping his approach to business and personal growth. This chapter highlights Onesimus's belief in the value of mistakes as learning opportunities and stepping stones to greater wisdom and success.

Onesimus openly discusses various missteps he has made throughout his entrepreneurial journey. These range from strategic business errors, such as misreading market trends or underestimating financial challenges, to interpersonal mistakes in managing relationships with partners, employees, or clients.

Central to this chapter is the concept that mistakes, while initially painful or costly, are invaluable learning experiences. Onesimus reflects on how each mistake provided him with deeper insights into the workings of business, human nature, and his own strengths and weaknesses. He shares how he has learned to embrace a mindset of continuous learning, where the focus is not on avoiding mistakes but on extracting valuable lessons from them.

This chapter also explores how Onesimus implemented changes based on his past mistakes. He adjusted his business strategies, improved his decision-making processes, and adopted more effective communication and management practices. These changes were not just reactive measures but proactive steps toward personal and professional improvement.

One of the key messages of "Learning from Past Mistakes" is the importance of resilience and the ability to bounce back from errors. Onesimus emphasizes that mistakes should not define or derail one's journey but should be used as catalysts for growth and improvement. He advocates for a culture where mistakes are openly acknowledged and discussed, rather than hidden or ignored, to foster an environment of transparency and continuous improvement.

"Learning from Past Mistakes" is a testament to Onesimus's maturity, humility, and wisdom. It underscores his ability to turn setbacks into success stories and demonstrates his commitment to lifelong learning and self-improvement. This chapter serves as an inspiration to entrepreneurs and individuals alike, showing that the path to success is often paved with lessons learned from past mistakes.

THE PATH OF A SERIAL ENTREPRENEUR

"The Path of a Serial Entrepreneur" is an expansive chapter in Onesimus Malatji's narrative, chronicling his journey as a serial entrepreneur who has ventured into multiple businesses across various industries. This chapter explores the dynamism, adaptability, and perpetual drive that characterizes Onesimus's approach to entrepreneurship.

Onesimus's journey as a serial entrepreneur is marked by his continuous search for new opportunities and challenges. He is driven not just by the pursuit of financial success but by a genuine passion for exploring new ideas and creating innovative solutions to problems. This chapter delves into the diverse range of businesses he has started or been involved in, from technology and telecommunications to publishing and mentorship programs.

A key theme in this chapter is the unique set of skills and qualities that Onesimus possesses and develops as a serial entrepreneur. This includes an ability to quickly learn and adapt to different industries, an aptitude for risk assessment and management, and a knack for recognizing market trends and gaps. Onesimus's journey demonstrates his flexibility in thinking and his willingness to pivot strategies or enter entirely new markets.

The narrative also touches on the challenges and complexities of managing multiple ventures simultaneously. Onesimus discusses the importance of effective time management, delegation, and building reliable teams. He shares insights into how he balances his involvement across different businesses while ensuring each venture receives the attention and resources it needs to thrive.

"Onesimus's Path as a Serial Entrepreneur" also reflects on the personal satisfaction and fulfilment he derives from his entrepreneurial ventures. For Onesimus, the journey of building various businesses is as rewarding as the successes they achieve. He views each venture as an opportunity to learn, grow, and contribute positively to society.

This chapter is a celebration of the entrepreneurial spirit, showcasing Onesimus's relentless pursuit of new business horizons and his ability to navigate the challenges and rewards of serial entrepreneurship. It serves as an inspiration and a guide for aspiring entrepreneurs, highlighting the possibilities that arise from passion, resilience, and a willingness to continuously explore new opportunities.

FACING UNCERTAINTY WITH COURAGE

"Facing Uncertainty with Courage" is a compelling chapter in Onesimus Malatji's entrepreneurial journey, portraying his resolve and bravery in the face of the unknown and unpredictable aspects of business and life. This chapter underscores the inevitable presence of uncertainty in entrepreneurship and Onesimus's approach to confronting it with a blend of courage, wisdom, and strategic foresight.

Throughout his various business endeavours, Onesimus has repeatedly encountered situations fraught with uncertainty. These ranged from fluctuating market conditions and technological disruptions to unexpected financial challenges and personal setbacks. In this chapter, Onesimus shares how he navigates these uncertain waters, maintaining his direction and purpose despite not always knowing what lies ahead.

A key element of this chapter is Onesimus's mindset when dealing with uncertainty. He views it not as a deterrent but as an inherent part of the entrepreneurial journey. Onesimus emphasizes the importance of embracing uncertainty, understanding that it often leads to innovation, growth, and new opportunities. He adopts a proactive approach, staying flexible and adaptable, ready to pivot strategies as situations evolve.

Onesimus also discusses the role of courage in facing uncertainty. For him, courage is not the absence of fear but the ability to move forward in spite of it. He highlights the importance of taking calculated risks, trusting his instincts, and learning to be comfortable with not having all the answers. Onesimus believes that facing uncertainty with courage is essential for any entrepreneur who wishes to break new ground and achieve significant milestones.

The chapter further delves into practical strategies for managing uncertainty. Onesimus shares his techniques for risk assessment, scenario planning, and maintaining a strong support network, which includes mentors, peers, and advisors who provide diverse perspectives and guidance.

"Facing Uncertainty with Courage" is a testament to Onesimus Malatji's strength of character and his unwavering commitment to his entrepreneurial vision. It showcases his ability to confront the unknown with confidence and determination, serving as an inspiration for entrepreneurs and individuals alike. This chapter underscores the message that while uncertainty is an unavoidable aspect of life and business, it can be met with resilience, courage, and a forward-looking attitude.

THE ART OF REINVENTION

"The Art of Reinvention" is a dynamic and inspiring chapter in Onesimus Malatji's entrepreneurial narrative, focusing on his ability to continually adapt and transform himself and his businesses to stay ahead in the ever-changing landscape of the modern world. This chapter delves into the concept of reinvention, both as a personal and business strategy, showcasing Onesimus's knack for evolving in response to new challenges and opportunities.

Onesimus's journey is marked by a series of reinventions. In business, he has navigated through various industries, constantly adapting his strategies, embracing new technologies, and venturing into unexplored markets. Each reinvention is a response to market changes, technological advancements, or lessons learned from past experiences.

This chapter also explores the personal aspect of reinvention. For Onesimus, reinvention is not just a business necessity but a personal philosophy. He believes in the power of continuous learning, self-improvement, and staying open to new ideas and perspectives. Onesimus shares his insights into how personal growth is intertwined with professional success, and how embracing change can lead to a more fulfilling and impactful life.

One of the key themes of "The Art of Reinvention" is the balance between maintaining one's core values and being flexible enough to adapt to new situations. Onesimus emphasizes the importance of staying true to one's fundamental principles and goals while being willing to change tactics, explore new ventures, or even radically shift one's business model when necessary.

Onesimus also addresses the challenges of reinvention, such as the risk of failure, the fear of the unknown, and the potential resistance from others. He discusses how he overcomes these challenges through careful planning, risk assessment, and cultivating a mindset that views change as an opportunity rather than a threat.

"The Art of Reinvention" is a compelling account of how adaptability, resilience, and a willingness to evolve are critical for long-term success and satisfaction in both business and life. This chapter serves as an inspiration and guide for individuals and entrepreneurs alike, demonstrating that the ability to reinvent oneself is a powerful tool in navigating the complexities and uncertainties of the modern world. For Onesimus, reinvention is more than a strategy; it's an art form that has enabled him to continually grow, innovate, and thrive in the face of constant change.

THE GIFT OF EMPOWERING OTHERS

"The Gift of Empowering Others" is a heartfelt and impactful chapter in Onesimus Malatji's story, highlighting his dedication to uplifting and empowering those around him. This chapter explores Onesimus's commitment to mentorship, community engagement, and creating opportunities for others, reflecting his belief in the power of positive influence and support.

Throughout his entrepreneurial ventures, Onesimus has not only focused on his own success but has also actively sought ways to empower others. This chapter delves into various initiatives and actions he has undertaken to share his knowledge, experience, and resources to benefit individuals, particularly aspiring entrepreneurs and community members.

One key aspect of this chapter is Onesimus's mentorship role. He takes great pride in guiding and nurturing young entrepreneurs, offering advice, sharing lessons from his own journey, and providing practical support where possible. Onesimus views mentorship as a two-way street, where he also gains fresh perspectives and stays connected with new trends and ideas.

Onesimus's approach to empowering others extends beyond mentorship. He engages in community projects and initiatives aimed at improving lives and providing opportunities for growth and development. Whether it's through sponsoring educational programs, supporting local businesses, or investing in community-led projects, Onesimus is committed to making a tangible impact.

The chapter also highlights how Onesimus creates empowering environments within his own businesses. He fosters a culture of learning, collaboration, and innovation, encouraging his team members to take initiative, develop their skills, and contribute their ideas. He believes that empowering his employees leads to a more dynamic, innovative, and successful business.

"The Gift of Empowering Others" reflects Onesimus's deep understanding that true success comes not just from personal achievements but from the ability to uplift others. This chapter is a testament to the impact that one individual can have through acts of mentorship, support, and empowerment. For Onesimus, empowering others is not just a responsibility; it's a rewarding and enriching experience that forms an integral part of his life and work. His actions inspire a ripple effect of positivity and development, showcasing the profound influence that empowering others can have on individuals, businesses, and communities.

LEAVING A LASTING IMPACT

"Leaving a Lasting Impact" is a profound and reflective chapter in the story of Onesimus Malatji, highlighting his dedication to creating a legacy that extends far beyond the conventional boundaries of business success. This chapter delves into how Onesimus, through his entrepreneurial ventures and personal actions, strives to leave a mark that positively influences not just the present generation but also future ones.

Onesimus's concept of a lasting impact is multifaceted. Professionally, it involves building businesses that are not only profitable but also sustainable and responsible. He focuses on ventures that address societal needs, promote ethical practices, and contribute to the community's well-being. His commitment to sustainable business practices is a testament to his desire to leave the world better than he found it.

In addition to his business endeavours, Onesimus places significant emphasis on mentorship and knowledge-sharing. He understands that by nurturing and guiding young entrepreneurs, he can extend his impact far into the future. Onesimus invests his time and resources in developing the next generation of leaders, sharing his experiences and lessons to help them avoid the pitfalls he encountered and capitalize on emerging opportunities.

The chapter also explores the personal values and principles that guide Onesimus in his quest to leave a lasting impact. He lives by the belief that success is measured not just by personal achievements but also by the ability to uplift others. His actions are driven by a deep sense of responsibility to his community and a commitment to making a positive difference.

"Leaving a Lasting Impact" is a reflection of Onesimus Malatji's holistic view of success and legacy. It highlights his belief in the power of responsible entrepreneurship and the role of business leaders in driving social change. This chapter is an inspiring reminder of the profound impact that one individual can have and the ripple effect of positive actions. For Onesimus, leaving a lasting impact is about creating a legacy that transcends business achievements, encompassing a life lived with purpose, integrity, and a commitment to the greater good.

REFLECTIONS ON A LIFE'S JOURNEY

"Reflections on a Life's Journey" is a deeply introspective and poignant chapter in Onesimus Malatji's narrative, where he takes a moment to look back and reflect on the path he has traversed in his life and career. This chapter is a compilation of insights, lessons learned, and wisdom gained from a journey marked by both triumphs and trials.

In this reflective space, Onesimus contemplates the various phases of his life - from his early beginnings and the challenges he faced, through the numerous entrepreneurial ventures, to his current state of personal and professional maturity. He considers the pivotal moments that shaped his character, influenced his decisions, and directed the course of his life.

A key theme of this chapter is gratitude. Onesimus expresses deep appreciation for the experiences that have enriched his life, acknowledging both the people who have supported him along the way and the hardships that have taught him valuable lessons. He sees every encounter and event as a meaningful part of his life's tapestry.

Onesimus also shares his thoughts on the evolving meaning of success and fulfilment. He reflects on how his definition of success has shifted over time, moving from a focus on material achievements and recognition to a broader perspective that includes making a positive impact on others, finding personal contentment, and contributing to the greater good.

This chapter also delves into Onesimus's hopes and aspirations for the future. While he cherishes his past experiences, he looks forward with optimism and a willingness to continue growing, learning, and contributing. He talks about passing on his legacy, not just in terms of business achievements, but in the values, knowledge, and spirit of resilience and generosity that he embodies.

"Reflections on a Life's Journey" is a thoughtful and inspiring conclusion to Onesimus Malatji's story thus far. It is a reminder that life is a continuous journey of discovery and evolution. This chapter encourages readers to reflect on their own journeys, to find value in every experience, and to approach the future with hope and openness. For Onesimus, reflecting on his life's journey is an opportunity to acknowledge where he has been, understand where he is, and envision where he still wishes to go.

BEYOND THE ASHES: A NEW DAWN

"Beyond the Ashes: A New Dawn" is an evocative and forward-looking chapter in Onesimus Malatji's narrative, symbolizing his ability to rise from adversity and embark on a renewed path with fresh perspectives and revitalized aspirations. This chapter signifies a rebirth of sorts, where Onesimus emerges from the metaphorical ashes of past challenges to greet a new dawn of possibilities and opportunities.

In this chapter, Onesimus reflects on how his experiences, particularly the setbacks and struggles, have been instrumental in shaping a new phase of his life and career. He discusses how overcoming these challenges has not only made him more resilient but also more insightful about his purpose and goals.

Onesimus shares his renewed vision for the future, which encompasses both his professional endeavours and personal aspirations. Professionally, he is poised to venture into new business territories, applying the lessons learned from his past experiences to build more sustainable and impactful enterprises. He talks about harnessing the latest technologies and innovations to create ventures that not only succeed commercially but also contribute positively to societal needs.

Personally, Onesimus emphasizes a deeper commitment to his own well-being and to nurturing the relationships that matter most to him. He speaks about the importance of work-life balance, maintaining health and wellness, and investing time and energy in his family and community.

The theme of "new dawn" in this chapter also reflects Onesimus's ongoing commitment to growth and learning. He remains open to new ideas, ready to adapt to changing circumstances, and enthusiastic about continuing his journey of personal and professional development.

"Beyond the Ashes: A New Dawn" is a chapter full of optimism and hope. It illustrates that from the ashes of hardship and failure can emerge new strength, wisdom, and opportunities. Onesimus's story in this chapter serves as an inspiration, encouraging readers to always look beyond the present challenges to the potential of a new and brighter dawn. It's a testament to the enduring spirit of renewal and the endless possibilities that await on the horizon of every life's journey.

THE ULTIMATE ASCENT: LOOKING FORWARD

"The Ultimate Ascent: Looking Forward" is a visionary and aspirational chapter in Onesimus Malatji's narrative, marking a phase of proactive growth and forward-thinking in his life and career. This chapter encapsulates Onesimus's outlook toward the future, characterized by ambitious goals, renewed energy, and an unwavering commitment to reach new heights in both his personal and professional endeavours.

In this chapter, Onesimus shares his vision for the future, which is not just an extension of his past achievements but a significant leap forward. He talks about setting new, more challenging goals for his businesses, exploring untapped markets, and leveraging cutting-edge technologies to drive innovation and growth.

A key theme of "The Ultimate Ascent" is Onesimus's dedication to continuous improvement and lifelong learning. He emphasizes the importance of staying curious, keeping abreast of industry trends, and constantly acquiring new skills. This mindset of growth and adaptability is what propels Onesimus to aim for higher achievements and to view the future as a landscape of limitless possibilities.

Onesimus also reflects on his role as a leader and mentor in this chapter. He envisions himself not just as a business leader but as a community influencer, sharing his experiences and insights to inspire and guide the next generation of entrepreneurs.

He talks about the responsibility that comes with his successes and how he plans to use his influence to foster positive change and empowerment.

Personal growth and fulfilment continue to be a significant focus for Onesimus as he looks forward. He speaks about balancing his professional ambitions with his personal life, ensuring that his journey toward the ultimate ascent is holistic and enriching. Onesimus's commitment to his family, health, and personal well-being remains as strong as his business aspirations.

"The Ultimate Ascent: Looking Forward" is a chapter full of optimism and strategic planning. It showcases Onesimus Malatji's dynamic approach to the future – one that is grounded in realism but elevated by ambition and hope. This chapter is a powerful reminder that the journey of growth and success is ongoing and that the future holds new mountains to climb and horizons to explore. For Onesimus, the ultimate ascent is not just a goal but a continuous journey of reaching higher, pushing boundaries, and envisioning a future filled with achievement and fulfilment.

EPILOGUE

As we reach the epilogue of Onesimus Malatji's extraordinary journey, we find a narrative that is far from concluding. Instead, it's a pause, a reflective moment in an ongoing story of resilience, innovation, and the relentless pursuit of growth and fulfilment.

Onesimus's journey, chronicled through the various chapters of his life, is emblematic of the entrepreneurial spirit in its purest form. It's a tale of rising and falling, learning and leading, challenging the status quo, and relentlessly pushing the boundaries of what's possible. Onesimus's story is not just about the successes and failures of a businessman; it's about the evolution of a visionary, a leader, and a mentor.

In this epilogue, Onesimus stands as a figure of inspiration and a testament to the power of perseverance. His life's work goes beyond the enterprises he has built; it extends into the lives he has touched, the communities he has empowered, and the positive changes he has fostered in the world around him.

Looking ahead, the future for Onesimus is a canvas of potential, filled with new ventures, unexplored opportunities, and continued contributions to the world of entrepreneurship. He remains committed to his path of lifelong learning, always open to new ideas and ready to embrace the next challenge.

As we close this chapter of his story, Onesimus Malatji's journey continues to inspire those who dream big, who face challenges head-on, and who tirelessly work to make a difference in their world. His story is a reminder that the path of entrepreneurship is as much about the journey as it is about the destination, and that true success comes from the impact one leaves on the world and the legacy that endures.

The epilogue of Onesimus's story is an open-ended invitation to all aspiring entrepreneurs and dreamers: to embark on their journeys, to embrace their paths with courage and resilience, and to contribute their unique chapters to the world's ever-unfolding story of innovation, growth, and transformation.

AFTERWORD

As we reflect on the journey of Onesimus Malatji, narrated through the chapters of his life, we find in his story a rich tapestry of lessons, inspirations, and insights. This afterword serves as a contemplative space to distil the essence of Onesimus's experiences and to consider the broader implications of his journey for aspiring entrepreneurs and individuals seeking to make their mark in the world.

Onesimus's story is one of resilience in the face of adversity, innovation amidst challenges, and the relentless pursuit of growth and self-improvement. His journey underscores the fact that the path to success is rarely linear. It is filled with obstacles, learning opportunities, and moments of self-discovery. Onesimus's ability to adapt, to rise from setbacks, and to constantly reinvent himself stands as a guiding beacon for anyone navigating the uncertain waters of entrepreneurship.

His commitment to empowering others and giving back to the community highlights a crucial aspect of leadership often overlooked in traditional business narratives. Onesimus demonstrates that true success is measured not just in profit margins and market shares, but in the positive impact one has on the lives of others. His mentorship, community involvement, and dedication to fostering positive change are as much a part of his legacy as his business achievements.

The afterword also invites readers to reflect on their personal definitions of success and fulfilment. Onesimus's journey encourages us to look beyond conventional metrics and to consider how our professional and personal lives can intertwine to create a holistic and satisfying life journey.

Finally, the story of Onesimus Malatji is a testament to the entrepreneurial spirit's enduring power. It's a reminder that with passion, resilience, and a willingness to learn and grow, every challenge can be transformed into an opportunity for advancement and every setback can become a stepping stone to greater achievements.

As we conclude the narrative of Onesimus Malatji, his story continues to resonate and inspire. It stands as an enduring narrative of the power of the human spirit to overcome, to evolve, and to impact the world profoundly. The afterword is not just a closing remark but an invitation to each reader to embark on their journey of discovery, growth, and impact.

~~~~~~~~~~~~~~~**END**~~~~~~~~~~~~~~~~~

www.ingramcontent.com/pod-product-compliance
Lightning Source LLC
Chambersburg PA
CBHW021110080526
44587CB00010B/461